THE
W.O.W
EFFECT

ANITA FAYE WILSON

THE W.O.W EFFECT
Anita Faye Wilson

979-8-9884334-0-8 Paperback
979-8-9884334-1-5 Digital
Library of Congress Catalog Number: 2023910070

Cover and Interior Design by: Charlyn Samson

Pecan Tree Publishing
www.pecantreebooks.com

New Voices | New Styles | New Vision –
Creating a New Legacy of Dynamic Authors and Titles
Hollywood, FL

DEDICATION

---

*T*HIS BOOK IS DEDICATED to my mother Elmar Green for believing the report of the Lord and allowing me to live. Even though you have taken your wings, your legacy will live on. Mama, I did it!

ACKNOWLEDGEMENTS

𝒟EAR GOD. YOU HAVE allowed me to put into words my journey through a lifetime of affirmations and declarations. I didn't understand it as a child, but when I learned the power behind my spending countless hours in the mirror encouraging myself, I was able to use it to navigate through some of life's toughest storms. Writing this book allowed me to heal from a lifetime of suppressing negativity. You guided me through every chapter so I could help others learn how to re-optimize their minds and use the power of positive words to evolve and grow. This is only the beginning. I'm far from done sharing my stories. Thank you, God, for reminding me that I have the power to live an abundant, drama free life. Every trick the devil tried hasn't worked. He won't stop trying, and his tricks will still never work. I will continue to triumph over him by the blood of the Lamb and by the word of my testimony. (Revelation 12:11)

Dear family. I would not be who I am if I hadn't been in the lineage chosen by God for me. I'm grateful for my parents, the late Elmar Green and Frank Green; my siblings Alveda, Carrie, Constance, Frank (deceased), Anthony, Timothy (deceased) and my bonus brother Vincent. You all are the backbone to my existence. Thank you. I can't leave my fur baby Zeus out. You left us right before this book was published. Thank you for blessing us with your charm and love for nine incredible years.

To Kyle who I raised and nurtured. I did my best to give you a life worth living. To ALL my nieces and nephews, and cousins galore. Too many of y'all. The Cooks sure do multiply. I appreciate all of you.

To my extended family who have made this life so much easier knowing that you love me and have my back. Valerie, Melissa, Annette, Brenda, Lorraine, Rosalyn, Snovia, Danielle, Sandye, Joe, Glenda, Susan, and Athena, you all are some of the most amazing people. My life is so much better with you in it.

Dear Claudette. Thank you for pushing me and not letting me forfeit this purpose. God knows exactly who to put into your life with the skills and expertise to pull out your best. You are a gift. Even when I wanted to quit, you wouldn't let me. I appreciate you so much.

For all of you who pick up this book, open it and read it from cover to cover, I pray your life is forever changed. Who knew that 15 years ago God would give me a gift I didn't realize I had. He blessed me with the power to encourage and uplift others with words. I started doing online affirmations during my own storms to soothe my deepest hurts and pains. Encouraging others somehow encouraged me. I started this in 2008. Ten years later, I received a revelation about what the tag line attached to my affirmations meant and I started to write about it. Then five years after living the last portion of this book, God showed me that by my double grace birthday, 55, this season would be complete; and I could allow others to embrace an anecdote that will undoubtedly heal wounds and change your mindset. Now you can get the full anecdote. Words Optimize Wholeness.

I pray the words on these pages make you healthy, whole and give you peace. WOW! Be Blessed and Be Free!

ABOUT THE AUTHOR

*A*NITA FAYE WILSON IS known for being passionate about two things – Ministry and Music. The youngest of seven children born to the late Frank Green and Elmar Green in Daytona Beach, FL. Wilson always knew she would travel the world, see remarkable places, and do amazing things. She spent most of her young years sharing the stage with many music industry greats including Betty Wright, Gloria Estefan, and Whitney Houston. Later she started working behind the scenes as a vocal coach, artist developer and music industry consultant and has shaped and molded the careers of some of the most successful artists on the charts.

Wilson was called into the ministry in 1995. Throughout her life she maintained her driving force in the two areas of passion without compromise. She has served as an Associate Minister in some of the most prominent megachurches in Florida holding positions like Minister of Music, Pastor of

Women, Dean of Bible College, etc. With all these momentous events in her life, Anita Faye Wilson still felt like there was still more. Being so full of ideas, dreams, and visions, it is no wonder Wilson would find herself flowing with every shift of the paradigm in her life while hearing the words that are so applicable to her, "To whom much is given, much is required." And so, the vision continues.

In 2018, on the heels of a transition in her life, Wilson answered yet another clarion call to step out into the deep and share her story. A story that would shed light on a gift that was always a part of her, though she did not realize its impact. The ability to dream and speak your dreams into existence is a tool that can change the course of people's lives. After looking back over her life and giving account of many instances where she saw herself speak life into dark moments, Wilson saw exactly what she was destined to do at 50 years old. She became an author and a transformational coach, launching her coaching services, where she helps others to define their purpose through the power of positive words.

Movement Worldwide, Inc./The M.O.V.E.M.E.N.T was launched in 2018. Movement Worldwide is a Motivational Organization Veered to Educate Minds Empower Nurture and Transform. Subsequently through the process of dealing with her personal journey toward better health, with the help of three friends, she launched Eat Well Live Well Be Well LLC, a health and wellness coaching business that helps individuals learn to take controls of their health by educating them to make better choices regarding food and supplemental health care.

This 2019 recipient of the Cultural Educator Award from the Broward County Chapter of United Nations Foundation, continues to thrive as a Music Manager and Consultant, shaping and molding the lives of many of the Music Industry's greatest of our time. And she also keeps true to her calling motivating and transforming the lives of people through private coaching, online classes, and seminars, and through public speaking.

FOREWORD

$\mathcal{I}$STILL VIVIDLY REMEMBER THE day. My uncle, his mocha-toned, nearly bald head gleaming under a hot Georgia sun was standing by a fenced in area. He was soothing a horse and I stood several feet away from the area because horses and I do not mesh. We have a mutual understanding. I stand away from them. They won't act crazy in my presence.

My uncle turned to me and said, "Claudie, I owe you an apology."

"Apology?" I inquired. "For what?"

"Because I didn't peg you right. 'Cause you were always so quiet and in your own world, I thought you weren't going to be much of anything. But you doing allright for yourself."

I was floored. Honestly, I wanted to burst into a full-on hollering crying fest. I was in my late 20s at the time and killing it in my radio news production career. To hear those words crushed me. Instead, I burrowed my forehead and held my hand against it to shield my eyes from the sun, looked at him and said, "I appreciate your apology. Who knew being quiet meant being nothing."

He did go on to apologize again, admitting he was wrong for thinking that way. What his truth revealed to me though was there were some words being spoken about me in the family and I wondered if that is why I was always handled with the spoons no one else would cook with. (Know what I mean?) They had released words into the atmosphere about me and they could not see me beyond the expectations and the assignments of their words.

Sadly, I took on that practice of errantly assigning negative words and stories and beliefs about me for years. Never thinking I was as smart, as pretty, as good, as worthy as others in my life and in my circles. Never believing anything I achieved was good enough. That taunting truth would pierce me again when I was selected to win a community award for my writing work while I was employed at a radio station, however, fearing the award would leave fellow employees who were not literary creatives slighted, some secret wrangling meant an award meant for me – individually, was becoming a group award. Although, I was secretly given a heads up about the change privately, I was devastated. In one behind-the-scenes move I was told (in action) that I was not worthy enough in my accomplished works to be applauded alone. One of the things I had spoken over my life came back to slap me – hard! I took my certificate, got to my car as quickly as I could and cried.

Words, as the late author Ntozake Shange said, "live, breathe and move." They are energetic. Thus, they can be tools or weapons. They can be explosive or embracing. They can be insightful or insulting. What you speak them to be they will become. If you have trained your words to be weapons in your life, until you transform what you allow to be spoken to you, around you, over you and into you – especially BY YOU – they will energetically bring you all that weaponry fire!

Anita Wilson and I have known each other for years. In an interesting season of adjustment that came simultaneously for both of us, we would often have to speak life into each other – often daily. Sometimes life simply sounded like, "Girl. You can get out of the car today. If you get out of the car, you've done good, and all will be well." During that season we were struggling under weaponized words spoken about us, so we had to be good medicine for each other. Anita's unfolding of the significance of the prescriptive words we must feed self is beyond engaging, it is food for your spirit, libation for your soul, old school do-wop R & B for your heart. Your mind will yell, "SING THEM GOOD WORDS. THOSE ARE MY JAM!

Listen. Speak joy! Speak peace! Speak wealth! Speak life! And then, as Anita declares, "BE FREE!"

E. Claudette Freeman

INTRODUCTION

THE W.O.W EFFECT
by

Anita Faye Wilson

*W*ORDS HAVE ALWAYS INFLUENCED me. Whether good or bad they affected me. Even when the words were coming out of my own mouth. I grew up as a kid with a very vivid and colorful imagination. Long before I knew the power of my words, I would dream up things and speak them into existence. I was so much of a dreamer; I would sit and have long conversations with myself about what "WE" were gonna do. Notice I said - we. Because I always felt like I was speaking to many others and sometimes massive crowds of people. But there was only me in the room. Now under normal circumstances, one would refer to me as slightly mentally imbalanced or borderline crazy. In my younger years, people would just ignore children like me and say things like, "She'll grow out of it." Honestly, I don't think my family was moved by it one way or the other. I wasn't afraid to speak my dreams aloud. I would share them with friends and family; anyone who would listen. Some would entertain me while others would giggle behind my back. I knew when they were with me. And, yes, I even knew when they weren't. Did it bother me? Sometimes. But it still didn't stop me from dreaming and speaking.

But there's a whole other side to words spoken. Growing up I was unusually talented for my age. I was considered a prodigy in my craft of singing. Now to me it was nothing special. It was just what came natural for me. This gift was so significant that I feel like I paid a special price for it. Yes, I have used my voice my entire life to support myself financially. But in some instances, it caused me grief. I was exceedingly popular because of it. Not all my popularity was positive though. There were some people who downright hated me because of my gifts and did everything they could to destroy me with their words. I started singing at an early age. It's something that I've done since as far back as I can remember. I'm talking about two or three-years old. When I was a small child people were kind to me. I would constantly hear words like "You're amazing! You sound so good to be so young! You're so talented. What a gifted young lady you are!" all having a positive effect on me. It made me want to sing more and more. I tried everything I could to get better and better. Hearing kind words was encouraging and motivating. But something different happened by the time I reached my puberty years. I remember being a student in the seventh grade. I was so excited to show my talents to everyone that I entered the school pageant. Every little girl wanted that crown. But I was determined it was gonna be mine! Prior to the pageant I got into an altercation with a popular boy at the school. He made advances towards me that made me uncomfortable, so I turned him away. A few days later was the opening night of the pageant. It was my first one ever! I had been waiting for this my whole life. There I was with all the other contestants performing our opening number. Each of us had to do a 10 second dance move when our name was introduced. We were all new to each other. I only knew a few people who were from my school zone. Everyone was super excited. The names were being called, "Contestant number 3!" and they would call out the name and the entire place would erupt in cheers. I couldn't wait. When my turn came to be introduced, I started to do my move, the crowd started to cheer. And then suddenly the disgruntled rejected young man and his friends started to loudly yell, "BOOOOOOO!" Yet with a painted-on smile, I continued to dance as if I heard nothing. After our performance, administrators got on the microphone and reprimanded the crowd for disrespecting the contestants and were warned not to boo any of us or they would face suspension. The pageant proceeded and we went into the talent division. The one thing I knew about myself was that no matter what the event was, I could always captivate an audience when I started to sing. I remember saying to myself backstage "Girl you are gonna tear this place up. They don't even know! And everybody who booed you is gonna want to be your friend. You'll see." There I was speaking to myself! The announcer calls my name. I walk out to the middle of the floor. More than one thousand eyes are on me. My whole family is there. I'm sure people were saying, "Isn't that the girl they booed?" I could hear people whisper. But I kept my cool. I had a knack for making the crowd completely still before I would sing. I wanted their undivided attention. I stood there amid the complete silence. You could hear a pin drop. Remember this was the contestant who had just been booed. So, everyone was waiting to see what she was really made of. I started to sing my own "churchy' rendition of "Tomorrow" from the musical Annie. Totally nothing like the original. By the time I got to "I just stick out my chin and grin and sayyyy..." The crowd was putty in my hands. Before I could finish the song, they were on their feet cheering and screaming and some were in complete awe. It was as if there had been two completely different people before the crowd. One they hated and one they loved. Standing ovation. It was so powerful, the announcer had to wait about five minutes to give the crowd time to simmer down.

The next day it was the talk of the school. We still had to have the final assembly and choose the reigning queen. The chatter around the school was, "did you hear about how Anita got booed?" There were some engaged in conversations about me as if I was responsible for what happened. Everyone was sharing their own versions of the story. As I passed some of the friends of the rejected young man in the halls, I was called Stupid, Ugly, No good." Each word stung like a bee. And then on the other hand, some were speaking the positive, pleasant things to and about me. Like, "You're amazing. I love your voice. You did great!" Boy did that soothe the stinging sensation from the negative slurs. There I was, 12 years old and in a very transitional stage of my life. For the first time realizing how words can alter the fabric of your thinking, and existence. It was years before I realized how words created the hills and valleys and the swerves in my life. Throughout my life I have constantly had to verbally affirm myself. It became a way of life for me. It was how I coped with being so popular. Because with popularity came both sides of the coin. I was hated for being talented and popular, and on the other side I was loved for being talented and popular. It's taken me decades to come to terms with a wealth of knowledge that started out as an imaginative little girl who would talk to herself and believe her own dreams. Now this was liberating.

The words we speak have power. Whether we're speaking to someone else or whether we're speaking to ourselves. The bible says the power of life and death are in the tongue. We must be careful what we speak. And it's also important that we understand that we were given the power and authority to "speak those things that are not as though they were." Now, we can hear this stuff for a lifetime. But when we've reached that moment where we feel like we have exhausted every measure in our ability to move past our present situation; something happens. When you dare to open your mouth and begin to speak life, something amazing happens. Your eyes open. Your mind opens. Your heart opens. You start to finally see what's been sitting in front of you your whole life. For me it goes all the way back to that little dreamer talking to herself. When I allowed my mind to open, I saw so vividly that everything I was talking to myself about then completely lines up with everything I envision now. My destiny has always been in front of me. I have not been living my best life. I see myself WINNING. And I want to share what I have learned; I want to open you up to a way of operating that has been available to us since the beginning. I call it The W.O.W. Effect. I want to show you how to WOW yourself out of a dark place. I want to show you how to WOW yourself onto a path of healing and worth. I want you to learn how to WOW yourself onto the road to your destiny. I spent most of my life not realizing what my words can do. I grew up the youngest child in a very Christian home. My mother quoted scripture every day. I would always hear people say stuff like "You have power in your tongue!" Of course, I as a child took it. But as I grew older, I understood the actual meaning, but it didn't quicken in me until I had to WOW myself to life again.

WORDS PLANT SEEDS

*E*VER SINCE I COULD remember, I would hear my mother give the testimony of my birth. She called me her "miracle baby". I could feel it coming. I would be sitting on the church pew of this old building built by the hands of the people sitting in it. Even my mom who often made mention that she climbed on top and helped build the roof. There I am swinging my legs back and forth. I can still see my little socks folded around my ankles with the ruffle trim. And I'd hear my mom say, "Stand up Faye!" The church would erupt in praise. She would say, "Now this is my miracle baby." She would tell the story of how shortly after I was conceived, the doctors told her she was diagnosed with pancreatic cancer and that the cancer was killing her and me. So, she needed to have an abortion to start chemotherapy treatments. Now let me pause here for a moment. My mother was carrying her seventh child. She and my father had been married for many years. I came along as a complete surprise. She was facing her medical doctor who spoke finite words over not only her life, but also the life of her unborn seed. There I am, in a cocoon, the size of an avocado. Rarely developed enough for the doctor to hear a pulse. I'm just entering the second trimester where the fingers and toes begin to have definition. The eyelids, eyebrows, eyelashes, nails, and hair develop. Bones and teeth are getting denser. Even at that state I faced rejection. Someone was speaking words over me trying to diminish my existence even before I was born. Now my mother could've taken the doctor's advice and followed through to try to save her own life. But she was a woman of faith. She was a woman of prayer. And I have heard her say many times that she stood on the promises of God's word. She would shout, "Who's report will you believe!" to the top of her lungs. She rebuked those foul words and chose to believe God. She spoke life! Thank you, mama.

Something starts to happen when you grow up hearing something recited repeatedly. Words are like seeds. They plant into whatever they're spoken over. A seed can't grow unless it's planted in the right conditions. Sometimes this happens on purpose, and sometimes a seed could just fall to the ground and somehow ends up under enough soil and grows because the conditions are conducive for it. Seeds germinate in a cool dark place. It's in a hidden space where it takes root. That's how words process. When words are spoken to you it goes into your hearing and lodges in your memory. That's an inner space or dark space. In your memory is where the hidden secrets of the things you've heard are.

I want to share a story with you about how powerful words are. I have a friend who said he didn't talk until he was four. The whole family thought there was something wrong with him. He had gone from the baby gibberish stages to complete silence. For about a year or two he would only do hand gestures and head nods. I remember hearing his mother talk about how she was the only one who could really communicate with him. I could imagine it was frustrating for the rest of the family. But they had a language that only a mother could understand. Then finally one day the moment happened. The family had been out running errands. Mom and four kids came home and started unloading the car of groceries and all the items they had bought that day. They walked into their big country family home and greeted their father who had just come in from a long day's work. Everyone branches off to be about their own affairs. Mom is in the kitchen cooking dinner; the older kids are playing in the family room in the back of the house. And the little four-year-old boy is sitting in the front of the house, watching cartoons. Dad walks from the master bedroom into the room where the little boy is sitting. As he passes through, he looks at him and says, "If your momma asks where I went, tell her I'm running to the store, and I'll be back indirectly." Now remember, this is the kid who had never spoken. I'm sure dad wasn't really thinking about who he was talking to. I'm sure he wasn't aware that his message might not be relayed. This kid had never had verbal conversations with anyone. So, he walks out the door and gets into his old farmer's truck and drives off. The kid innocently sits there and continues to watch television. Mom is humming and getting dinner started to feed her family. She was a short petit woman. The kitchen had a lot of shelves too high for her to reach. It was a very normal thing for her to need the help of her husband who stood six-foot three towering over her tiny five-two frame. She realized she needed something from the top shelf of the pantry. But she can't reach it. As she would normally do, she calls for her husband not knowing he stepped out. She yells his name...he doesn't answer. She walks past the kid in the living room to the master bedroom and calls his name. Nothing. She walks through the living room past the four-year-old

again and out the front door and calls his name. Nothing! She walks past the kids again to the back door and yells his name in the back yard. Nothing! She comes back into the house from the backyard, walks into the family room and asks the other kids, "Hey! Have you seen your father?" "No!" they answer. So, she gets tired of looking and decides to get a ladder and get it herself. There she is in the garage searching for the ladder amongst the rakes and shovels. I could see the steam coming out of her nose. Because now she must drag this dirty ladder into the kitchen to get something that she could've easily had her husband get. She grudgingly drags the ladder in while mumbling under her breath. And voila! Mission accomplished.

About 20 minutes later, the father pulls up into the driveway in his old farmer's truck. He enters the house, passes the same kid, and pats him on the head and says, "Is everything alright son?" The kid nods his head yes. He walks through the house into the kitchen and notices there's a ladder in the middle of the floor. Meanwhile mom is still mumbling under her breath. She's angry because she had to interrupt her cooking time to do something that would've been so easy for his tall frame to do. So clearly seeing that mom has an attitude, dad treads lightly but is curious. So, he asks, "Why is this ladder in the kitchen?" I guess you can imagine that mom hit the ceiling.

She starts slamming pots and pans around. Every word from her mouth is accompanied by the slam of a dish. So, the boy slides off the sofa to see what the commotion is. He sees his parents engaged in a heated discussion. "I was looking for you everywhere," mom says. "I checked the rooms! I checked the back yard and the front yard. I didn't' know where you were. The kids didn't know where you were. "Dad says, "I told this boy that if you ask for me tell you I'm gone to the store!" Mom was like, "Really! No wonder!" knowing that the kid never spoke. Because remember in the days of the family of the 60s and 70s, mom was in the house, and dad made the money. Well in most homes. And even when both were working people, it was mostly mom who tended to the kids. So, Dad was so clueless that he told the kid who didn't talk. And even with the mom's response, it STILL hadn't registered. So, the dad turns to the kid and says, "Didn't you see your mom looking for me?" The kid nodded again. Dad says, 'Well why didn't you tell her what I said?" At this very moment, somewhere from his hidden place in his memory bank comes these words "Because she didn't ask me." And there was mom and dad in shock and excitement at the same time. He SPOKE! Tears of joy streaming down their faces. They began to have a conversation with him for the very first time. Who knew this was coming? For his whole life, he'd heard people talking around him. He knew the words. He would nod and point and make gestures to communicate. So, words that he heard had taken root. The bible says, "For out of the abundance of the heart, the mouth speaks" And from that moment, words poured out like a fountain.

You may not think some of the words you hear influence you at the time. I can give an account of many things I've heard throughout my life that have come back later to either haunt me or help me. Even words that were not necessarily spoken to me or about me. But they were in my memory. Those words spoken went into the hidden place and started to germinate. And then they took root. When the roots start to grow and the plant is forming, it starts moving through the dark place in search for sunlight. Some words that have been spoken over us have been growing since childhood. So, the roots have spread and are extraordinarily strong. Now this applies to both positive words and negative words. I spent my entire life hearing my mother's testimony. The doctors said one thing and my mother refused to accept it. She spoke the opposite. And WON! Words have power. Words that are spoken over you replay over and over in your mind. Hearing her give that testimony told me one thing that I always knew to be true. That is that my life had a purpose. I was meant to be here. I grew up with the understanding that I had beat the odds. My existence means something because I was a miracle. I have always had an innate nature to "beat the odds" I never gave up. When I heard no, I would keep going until I got a yes. Knowing that has always been my motivation. So, when I found myself at yet another crossroads, I learned that the very thing I had struggled with all my life was what God was going to use for the next dimension of my life. I knew how to get in the mirror and talk myself out of pain and depression. I knew how to speak the opposite of anything negative spoken against me. If I believed I was supposed to have something, a job, a career path or whatever, I would begin to speak it into existence. I want to help you understand that this is it. This is what has been missing from your life. If you have picked up this book, then surely you have stepped into a place in your life where you see something bigger than your power. You don't know how you're going to make it happen. But you do know it's your purpose. And what's been missing is the right driving force to get you there.

CHAPTER 2

THE HEALTH STATUS OF WORDS

*H*OW DID I GET here? I've asked myself this question a lot. When it comes to physical health, our bodies give us so many warning signs before we reach a serious point that leads to crisis. The same thing happens to us mentally. We get all the warning signs, but don't take heed. I remember when my mother suffered a cardiac arrest in 2013. Until that point, she had been in charge of her own life, her health and everything. She was independent and just stepping into her golden years. When she had this sudden attack, me and my siblings were completely caught off guard. It was unexpected. We were thinking, where did this come from? Did we miss something? Is there something we could have done to prevent this? I remember one of the cardiologists telling us that this didn't just happen. He explained it had been happening for a while and that we must go back and look at the events leading up to the cardiac arrest and we would find the root of the problem. It wasn't until we got our hands on her medical history that we found that root. Unbeknownst to us, she had been diagnosed with congestive heart failure eight years prior to the cardiac arrest. From that time, her diet and activity needed to change. Now I'm sure she thought that what she was doing was the right thing. But after getting the knowledge about her condition I realize that for so long, she had been living on borrowed time. She was so far from her proper diet and exercise. And there we were saying "How did we get here?"

When I look at my own life patterns, I notice the same type of neglect I saw with my mother. If we look back at the events that lead to our own cardiac arrest experience, we will find the root of the problem. I missed it! In retrospect, I had warnings and red flags all around me. Like the cardiologist said, there's always a root to the problem. How did I miss it? Well, honestly, I didn't even know I was sick. I thought I was living a whole healed life because I knew how to talk myself into a better place. But I never dealt with what was at the root. Each battle got tougher because I was not dealing with the true diagnosis. I was only treating the symptoms. When you only treat the symptoms, you don't heal. I want to encourage you to go beyond the surface. That's where the freedom is. That's where healing is. After many years of suffering through the painful symptoms and side effects of toxic words, I finally figured out the diagnosis.

DIAGNOSIS:

Many of us are suffering from what I call "Toxic Word Syndrome". Toxic Word Syndrome is a condition caused by toxic words being spoken to, about or around you. Some symptoms are: Low self-esteem, Doubt, Fear, Second Guessing, Paranoia.

Often, we find ourselves overwhelmed by expectations. We can spend a lifetime painting the canvas of our lives according to someone else's vision of who we are. And then we wonder why it's impossible to fill in the color and make it live. Well perhaps you have not painted what you envisioned. You've painted how others see you. And then other times our minds are clouded by the negative thoughts we've been feeding our spirit for years. One tiny seed of doubt and fear can reap a vineyard of self-sabotage. When toxic words become a part of your daily thinking, they seep into your soul and strangle your possibility. It's hard to believe in yourself if you have been meditating on disastrous thoughts about your own vision. Everything that you will ever be or have or accomplish starts with what's in your mind. That's why we must clear out the toxicity and fill it with healthy words. We should meditate on positive thoughts and victorious expectations. We must change our surroundings and conversations and be careful of what goes into our hearing as well as what comes out of our own mouths.

A diagnosis is simply identifying a disease from its signs or symptoms. Even though I had the gift of gab, I didn't realize the signs. The main two were second-guessing and paranoia. Sometimes we spend years looking at ourselves through other people's eyes. The toxicity was that the negative words had harvested in my mind and caused me to develop a mental illness that created delusions of everyone being out to get me. I watched everyone around me with the side eye. You would think I would have developed a desire to be a loner. No, it created the opposite. Instead of becoming a loner, I allowed a lot of people in my inner space with the assumption that I don't trust them anyway, so I'm just gonna get what I need and be done. See how sick that sounds. The realistic part of all of this is that we're human. And when we allow people into our inner space, without realizing it, we let our guards down. And when we let our guards down, we can easily get hurt by the bitter onset of betrayal. We need to pay attention to the signs and symptoms. Ignoring them can cause the symptoms to continue to grow and compound. Therefore, leading you to a life full of pain and misery.

PAIN:

TWS can lead you to a place of physical and emotional destruction. When something is spoken out of your mouth, it has a power that supersedes your understanding. God in all His power spoke the words, "Let there be", and everything that came after that, still is. We are living off those words to this day. Sound travels from object to object all the way out into the universe. That's why it's important to watch what you release; because the enemy can latch on to things that come out of your mouth. Moreover, the words that lodge in your memory are on repeat. They play over and over and over again. It's like planting a beautiful flower garden that gets smothered out by weeds. Weeds are ugly and vicious. They hide the beauty. Weeds have no value. They can be poisonous and have thorns. And they have accelerated growth patterns and often will leave seeds to perpetuate their own kind. Weeds compete for space and nutrients. They block the good plants from sunlight and starve them to the point that they become prone to insects and diseases, leaving them sick and unfruitful. This is much like the pain of TWS. It clouds your thinking. You become unproductive and fall into a state of depression. It can affect your eating habits and cause you to gain or even lose an unhealthy amount of weight. It can cause you to have a heavy heart and broken spirit with no drive or motivation. That's the kind of pain we experience when our lives are invaded by outside opinions that become our daily thought processes. Sometimes this pain is so deep we don't realize where the root starts. And if we try to rip it out, it can leave a gaping bleeding hole in our soul. This is a real thing, and it can lead you to an early grave if you don't treat it.

PRESCRIPTION:

"Are there no healing ointments in Gilead? Isn't there a doctor in the house? So why can't something be done to heal and save my dear, dear people?" (Jeremiah 8:22) This passage really speaks to the level of pain I was feeling from my TWS symptoms. I needed an antidote that was not only going to soothe my symptoms but promote complete healing as well. Once I knew what I was suffering from, I had to go into my lab and create a treatment that was sure to heal and save me from the toxicity that was destroying me, my dreams, and my purpose. There is a balm in Gilead.

The treatment for Toxic Word Syndrome isn't something that you can just take one dose of and be done. No, it is a daily need. A supplement that's necessary for daily living. The Apostle Paul challenges us to present our bodies as living sacrifices daily and to renew our minds. How could I have missed this simple thing that I knew to do? When you're sick, it's difficult to make good judgment. Imagine having years of toxicity. I went into my lab and came out with a prescription that was sure to cure my illness. I call it The W.O.W Effect.

Toxic words had infiltrated my life and I was about to abort my purpose. Life was on the line. Not just mine, but yours too;

and everyone else whose hands hold this book or whose ears are receptive to my voice. We're like computers. We have so much information stored up in our conscious and subconscious. And sometimes we must optimize, rewrite, or rearrange our mental data to improve efficiency. Otherwise, the computer could malfunction. Optimization is an act, process, or method of making something, such as a design, system, or decision, as fully perfect, functional, or effective as possible.

The W.O.W Effect is Words Optimizing Wholeness. I had been using the word WOW for years not realizing it was the one word that could pave the way to my deliverance. Putting the right information in your mind and thoughts will improve your thinking and change what comes out of your mouth. This is when I really started to experience true healing. I want the same for you. Recognize that you are your best asset. If you are ready to live your best life, then you must go through self-optimization. TWS must go. It's time to prune away the weed infestation of toxic thoughts and words that crowd your thoughts and prevents the "sun" and "son" from shining on you. We must plant a new vineyard of positive words that build you up and speak life. You must engage in personal development, personal growth, self-improvement, and self-help, to excel. If you want to increase your potential, live your best life and WIN, then it is time to apply this balm that will heal your soul.

Toxic Words

Marriages/Love

Love relationships, whether marriage or dating, can be challenging. When in bliss, it's the most powerful experience you will ever have. Love is powerful in its nature. God loved us so much that he gave us His son. How powerful is that? When you're in a marriage/dating relationship, you spend much of your time with the person you're in the relationship with.

Being with someone that much takes a toll on your patience. Getting to know someone is eye opening. I've heard people say so much, "You never know someone until you live with them." This much is true. In the beginning I believe that most people spend a lot of time trying to be who the other person needs them to be instead of being themselves. Eventually, you become comfortable and then the dragons come out. However, we sometimes ignore all warning signs because our heads are in the clouds, and we don't want anything to interrupt the fantasy. Most little girls 'dreams are to grow up, get married, have babies, and live happily ever after. Most boys' dreams are to grow up, get a nice car, have lots of ladies, lots of money, and then one day settle down -maybe. That always makes me chuckle. Our society today is much different from the depiction of June and Ward Cleaver and their kids Wally and The Beaver. Many of us have never lived like The Waltons or The Huxtables. However, all of us at some point in our lives have had a significant other, a dating relationship or a marriage. And after the affirmations of love have simmered down; after the butterflies in your tummy stop fluttering; after you have stopped daydreaming about them all day, the real deal sets in, it takes work to keep it together.

The problems that occur in these types of relationships often stem from personality clashes and failure to deal with those clashes on impact. We let so much go without correction. We have differences of opinions and different value systems, and we bring all those differences together to cohabitate. Over time our disagreements become frequent, and our demands are overwhelming. Then we bottle up our feelings and suffer quietly. It's like a time bomb waiting to explode. And sometimes one or both people in the relationship have a short fuse. This makes matters even worse. We don't deal with the little issues upfront, and then they soon become bigger issues. Then come the little spats. After a series of little spats come the bigger spats. Then the bigger spats become arguments. Then the arguments become full blown fights. And if we're not careful, the fights become war. And if we don't ever deal with any of those levels, it can become abusive. Both physical and verbal abuse. Verbal abuse is an area that we really don't realize affects us as much as it does. We become so accustomed to brushing it aside, that we do not deal with the matter head on. We stay and take it for so long that we allow it to toxify our spirit. See in our minds, we can't let go because we're looking for the old status to show up again. We want the butterflies and the heart palpitations. We keep longing for the day to return like it was in the beginning. Well let me serve you notice; you can't keep going back to that starting point. Because then all you will be doing is repeating the same cycle and never moving forward. So, you're in it. And when you don't know how to deal with the cycle of life along with the stress of being with someone day after day, the only thing you know how to do is lash out with words. Words that cut deep. Words that sting and burn you to your core. Toxic Words.

I wish I had someone to tell me the hard truth about what we're unpacking in these pages years ago. I plunged into marriage at the tender age of 22. I was green and clueless about life, love, and marriage. Unfortunately, the marriage went down a road of destruction. We were a couple who didn't view much in life, the same. We clashed in every area and every subject. My views of what our marriage should be were far from his. My goals and future desires did not line up with his. WOW! Who knew? Did I ignore the gulf of differences beforehand? The red flags were waving exceedingly high and proud long before we said, "I do"! But that didn't stop me from doing exactly what I wanted to do. That's how we are sometimes. We ignore the signs, and we tell ourselves we can make it better as if we know more than God. There was so much toxicity present before the marriage, that it set up camp right there at the wedding. And it only got worse from there. It got so bad that sometimes I felt like a rag doll attached to a dart board,

Imagine this. You're at a shooting range. You are the target. Every word that comes out of the mouth of your significant other is like a bullet that rips through the fiber of the target. The target is still standing and intact. But there's a hole where the bullet penetrated. Being called out of your name on a constant basis tears holes in you just like that target. The words penetrate your mind, and soul. And there's a hole where it ripped into your psyche. You don't realize it right away, but you're not the same. Now you can take your target down after leaving the range and tape up the hole and all, but the evidence is still there. And then imagine going back repeatedly. It's like being a glutton for punishment. Well, what do you think the target is going to look like now? It's worse. There are more holes. And the more you shoot, the more holes. That's what TWS does. It rips apart your dreams and hopes of marital bliss. It leaves you shattered and broken trying to put the pieces back together. Here's another way of seeing it. If you shatter a vase repeatedly, it will never be as beautiful as it was when you first saw it on the shelf at the store. Eventually, it becomes very noticeable that it's been broken and glued back together. It loses its beauty and sparkle. The newness and the innocence are gone. It may still resemble the beautiful work of art it once was. But if you really look at it, you will see the flaws and the cracks. Now it looks tattered and worn. You are not fooling anyone with a painted-on smile. When your heart has been bruised over and over and when your countenance has been shattered by toxic words that are meant to rip you apart, it's difficult to hide the brokenness. The bigger the spat, fight, or war, the bigger the words. And then the words become phrases and the phrases become declarations. How much of this can you really take? How many bitches and whores can you be? How many times can you hear someone you love say they're leaving you because you don't make them happy? You're worthless. I hate being around you. Why did I ever marry you? Stings? Yes, it does. It rips the poor target to shreds. And then the shooter puts down his gun and leaves you hanging there broken. But somehow, we find the strength to pull out the tape and the glue.

We neglect ourselves by not dealing with the reason we're in the state we're in. So, we patch ourselves up and take that battered target that cracked vase to the next relationship. Not only do we see this problem in dating and marriage relationships, but also in business relationships, family relationships and friendships.

Business/Working Relationships

There's nothing more toxic than being on a job that you need to leave, and then having to be subjected to the toxicity of negative words being thrown at you. I didn't spend most of my life punching a clock for another employer. So, I have extraordinarily little corporate experience. But in my years, I've experienced enough to be able to share with you what a toxic working relationship can produce. I spent most of my adult life in business partnerships or just working for my own companies. But there's that 15-year window of time that I worked in various situations. I worked in full time ministry, which was a horse of a color I never imagined. Now don't get me wrong, I'm not against full time ministry work. But the truth of the matter is, it can be worse than the corporate world. You still must deal with bosses, people and the drama that comes along with it.

Let me talk about an employer/employee relationship. As with a marriage or a dating relationship, it starts off in bliss. You get up every day and skip off to your place of employment with pep in your step. Especially when you feel like you're working in your true purpose. Nothing feels better than getting up and going to work doing something you love. You feel liberated and accomplished. But human beings are flawed. We don't always manage things the right way. We see this in corporate America, in politics and in churches. Sometimes people in high positions carry themselves as if they have no accountability. I have always said that Christians tend to walk that thin line between our flesh and spirit. And during conflict we can very easily cross the line. I have had those moments in my life. As if this poor little target hasn't had enough, what did I do? Yep!

There it is that same old tired target. It already has holes in it from the marriage, or the friendship, or the dating relationship. And what do we do? We go to work and hang it up for more target practice. And we tell ourselves we're healed. Because what we do is, we take that same target down and patch up the holes. We do our best to make it look new. And here come the words. "You're poison. You have exhausted your worth here, but I'll let you continue to work. You are spiritually dead. No one will ever put you up front in their business after this." There were experiences in my life that led me from toxic relationship to toxic relationship, only to be broken repeatedly. Yet all I was doing was patching up the target and gluing the vase to continue the process. And to add insult to injury, I thought I had figured it out. Not only would I tape up the target, but I would also laminate it. Yes! That's really gonna work. See this is when we put up a wall and try to keep the target intact. This is only a defense mechanism, but it doesn't deal with the illness. Because when I took that same target into another situation, guess what happened. The bullets weren't penetrating as easily as before. Now I'm stronger. Right? WRONG! I didn't realize it, but I had only set myself up for stronger harsher words. This time instead of dealing with bullets, I was dealing with bombs and grenades. Because now, check out these words. "I will send you back wherever you came from. Your being here is like trying to put a square peg in a round hole. You're cursed! Your business is cursed! Everyone who does business with you is cursed!" Whoa! What a blow! Talk about weapons of mass destruction. At this point, the target is destroyed. I had to decide that enough is enough. This was my rock bottom.

In Love relationships, business relationships, family relationships, church relationships, etc.; we tend to carry the toxicity from one situation to the next. We don't take the time or the effort to deal with it at the moment. And over time we become a toxic individual incapable of producing. I talked about that beautiful garden in your heart and mind that became consumed by weeds. Weeds compete for space, block sunlight, and choke the life out of the good flowers. Weeds also regenerate and grow at a faster rate than the good stuff. So, there you are, one little lonely blossom amid ugly weeds with all those negative words for years and years just piling up and multiplying. Every now and then you muzzle up the strength to pull those weeds back long enough to breathe a little. You pull them back long enough to get a few rays of sunlight. You stretch your roots far enough to get just enough water to keep one little blossom going. And then you say, "See? I'm standing! Like that target full of bullet holes, like that vase shattered and glued over and over, like that lonely little blossom in the weeds, you are broken, bruised, and smothered. It's time to clean house.

We've got to go back to the basics and uproot what's contaminating our soil. Now you must be careful here. Some weeds have not germinated or sprouted yet. And some are so well mixed in that they appear to be good plants but they're in disguise. When you want to replant your garden, you must get your soil right. You must identify the weeds. You can't cultivate soil when you know you have an abundance of weed seeds. Remember, the weeds don't need your help. The seeds from the weeds fall to the ground and regenerate themselves. Those words in your spirit, in your heart and mind are on repeat. They're playing repeatedly and regenerating themselves.

The Real Battleground

Toxic words are not only the ones spoken about you, to you or around you, but also the ones spoken through you and by you. We must learn to watch our own mouth. When your mind is cluttered with toxic words, you will start to speak from what's inside you. For out of the abundance of the heart the mouth speaks. You must be careful not to speak defeat over your dream before it's even birthed. I have been so guilty of this. It took me a long time to realize that I had started to believe who other people said I was instead of looking at myself through God's eyes. You can't have your visions and dreams on the same focal point as negative and toxic words. It will blur your vision. You won't be able to see well enough to navigate through your journey. Therefore, the growth in our lives is stunted. We contaminated the growing area. You will not bear fruit if you don't take care of the process from the point of preparation. How can you expect a bountiful harvest of planted seeds in bad soil? I know it's difficult to face some of this stuff. Trust me, I have had to deal with some harsh realities of my own. I looked in the mirror and didn't like who I saw looking back at me. She was weak and frail. She was not living her best life. She was defeated and broken. She was pretending to be whole. She was putting on a face and dying inside. I looked at her and said, "This is not what you were created for! This is not who your mother risked her life for. Who are you? Why are you here? What about the dreams and the vision? What about your purpose? You were put here for a purpose and now it's time to figure things out." Everything starts in your mind. So, you must renew it. I have a cure for this condition. It's not easy. It's a process. It takes you facing hard truths and harsh realities. You must face your fears and doubts head on. But I can assure you this anecdote is one that you will never want to live without. You will keep this in your life's medicine cabinet forever.

C H A P T E R

HEART WORDS!

---

*W*HEN I GRADUATED FROM high school, I had big dreams of doing many things. I wanted to travel the world. I wanted to see things I had only seen in magazines and read about in books. My mom was a hard worker and did the best she could to take care of her family and instill values. She made sure we went on a family trip once a year, even if it was an hour down the road to a place called Silver Springs. And that was a big deal for us back in the day. Even though we knew what was around every corner of the entire theme park, it still felt great to just get away with family. My younger years were simple. It didn't take much to make me happy. But growing older came with an innate desire to have everything I had always dreamed about. As a young lady transitioning from high school to college, I had a vision for something different. I had a glimpse of possibility. It gave me a burning desire to go places and see things and do things that were just a dream for a girl where I came from. And most of the people I knew would never have the opportunity to do half of what I saw in my dreams. I wanted it bad!

This is the first time I began exercising the gift of positive words knowingly. As a child I did it, but as a young adult there was something different about it. About a year after high school, I ran into an old teacher who posed one question that put me in make-it-happen mode. When you know something is for you, you can't rest until you have it. I can remember, after seeing her, I went home and got in the mirror and said, "Now you know you have to make this happen!" I will get into what that was a little later.

The mirror is a powerful tool. If you stand there long enough, you will truly see yourself. And in most cases, you won't really like who you see. The way a mirror works is –photons, rays of light, coming from an object strike the smooth surface of a mirror, then bounce back at the same angle. Your eyes see these reflected photons as a mirror image. A mirror is made to reflect whatever it's facing. As people, we reflect on what we see. You can see this even in babies. They have a nature to mirror the mannerisms of what they see. I have endless videos of my niece Amori using gestures reflective of my mother who passed away while she was a toddler. She won't have vivid memories of her great grandmother, yet the mannerisms of my mother which she mirrors will stay with her for a lifetime.

I believe the most powerful observation I've had about the mirror was that I was able to change the image I saw with my words. When we look in the mirror our first instinct is to change something. We reposition our hair or apply more make up or fix our shirt to make it hang differently. The one thing that's certain is that you leave the mirror having made a change to something that was reflected.

When I look in the mirror, I look directly into my eyes. There's a metaphor – the eyes are the windows to the soul. Your eyes tell a lot about you. They change according to how you're feeling. When you're sad or angry, your eyebrows wrinkle causing your eyes to squint. And when you're happy or excited, you raise your eyebrows, which causes your eyes to open wider and become brighter. When you take the time and look, I mean really look, you see so much of what has not been said. This is the person you need to talk to in the mirror and, this is the person who needs to hear what I call "Heart Words".

When you have a dream and you know beyond the shadow of a doubt that you must see it through, your heart and mind become flooded with possibility. Culturally when one speaks about the heart, it refers to emotions. But biblically, it's much deeper than that. In both the Old and the New Testament, the word "heart" is used to describe the whole part of the innermost part of us. We have our mental which is the major part. This is where our actions and reactions process. We have our emotions, which are primarily brought on by thought, feeling and behavioral responses. And then we have our will, which is where decisions are made between the rational and emotive. So, when you see your dream and all your insides start to churn from all that is in you, the best thing to do is get it out before you explode. What better way to ration your thoughts than to talk them out? We must do something with those heart words. Heart words are full of passion and desire. Heart words are inquisitive, and they pique your curiosity. When you become pregnant with purpose and the baby is leaping in your belly, it invokes some type of response.

The bible says in Matthew 6:22-23 "The eye is the lamp of the body. If your eyes are healthy, your whole body will be full of light. But if your eyes are unhealthy, your whole body will be full of darkness. If then the light in you is darkness, how great is that darkness." The bible uses many metaphors particularly as it pertains to moral and ethical understanding. As I told you, the eyes usually tell the story from the soul. According to this scripture, we should be careful not to allow our inner light to grow dim. Think about this, when you look in the mirror into your eyes, you can really see the truth. Well, so can others. It's imperative that we get in the mirror and speak life daily so that our light would shine before men. For years, I thought I was fooling everybody. I'm sure you think the same. This personal development tool has brought so much deliverance and revelation to my life. My soul has been freed from darkness and captivity. This was one of the first signs that The WOW Effect was really working.

There's another passage of scripture in Second Corinthians 3:18 that says, "We all with unveiled face, beholding and reflecting like a mirror the glory of the Lord, are being transformed into the same image." We are walking mirrors people. A mirror is made to reflect whatever is in front of it. We as humans reflect what we see. Earlier in my ministerial days, I preached and taught about man in three dimensions, body, soul, and spirit. There are gateways through our flesh senses - sight, smell, hearing, taste, and touch. We have the soul realm where the senses from our flesh senses are gateways to our soul senses – imagination, conscious, memory, reason, and affection. From there are gateways to our spiritual senses

– faith, hope, reverence, prayer, and worship. But we have something between the soul and spirit. It's our will. And deep down in our inward parts, our hearts are often veiled. Veiled just as if there was a cloth hanging over the mirror. Are you showing the reflection of God's will or your will? Or is it the will of others for your life? Stings? I know. I had that experience with this revelation as well.

When I first accepted my calling as a mouthpiece for God, I had no idea what was on the horizon for me. I was young and had stepped into the middle of one of the most historic shifts in the Body of Christ. There was something new that God was doing. I was in the beginning of the third decade of my life. It was a very pivotal time. It was the time of a young woman's life where she realizes some of the errors of the past. When we get to a pivotal shift, the regret can send us into a mode that makes us say "I'm here now and I don't know how to get out of this." As for me, I stayed there and continued the spiral not realizing I was spiraling. There I was trying to become the picture of a preacher that I was told I was supposed to become. This was me living someone else's vision of who I was. And then the same hands that I thought were trying to build me up were also trying to tear me down. I call it my stormy weather season. Not the nice rain that waters everything and helps the fresh flowers to blossom and grow. No, I mean the vicious storms that uproot trees and cause major property damage. There were several things that happened in this season, a failed marriage, the loss of a child, isolation, attempted ministerial assassination, toxic relationships, or to borrow a phrase from my good friend and author and preacher Brenda L. Jackson, non-relationship relationships, deaths, depression, and I'm sure I'm leaving some out. Clearly my mirror was covered. There was not much of a great reflection showing from me. Whose reflection was I projecting? I look back and realize that what I was suffering from was a lingering case of Toxic Word Syndrome that had become viral. And they were deep rooted.

Some of them had lingered from childhood and some were current. The rest were my own words.

Toxic words are like dormant cancer cells. When they're dormant, they sit in what's called a quiescent state. It's a state of inactivity. It's there, but not causing trouble or symptoms. They stop diving and wait for the perfect environment for proliferation, which means to multiply. It is imperative that we deal with the toxicity within so that when we look into the mirror of our soul, we don't see all the negative descriptive language about who we are, but that we can see ourselves through God's eyes. The negative words are not an accurate representation of who you are. True affirmation will start to erase the negativity and unveil the truth about who we really are. Work on your heart words. Store up more heart words. Speak heart words and live heart words. Instead of wasting time worrying about things you can't change, start filling your heart with the words that bring life to those areas. Don't feed the toxic cells. Your heart words can kill them. Start going after the ones that are dormant. You in your flawed physical state can't change your situation, but God gave you the power to speak those things that are not as though they were. And when we do that with firm belief, things change

Get in the mirror and talk about your dreams. A pregnant woman must take care of her body because it's housing a life that must be birthed into the world. This is how you need to look at your dreams. The baby inside a pregnant woman is not just for her to dream about and feel leaping inside her. No, that life is meant to bless other people. What you have inside is meant to be a blessing to others as well. You're holding the key to someone's deliverance or to someone's future. So, get your heart in order.

You see, the mirror is not your enemy. Use this tool to reconnect with yourself. We lose ourselves in the self-pity and doubt brought on by the falsehoods of toxic verbiage. We also live in fear of the unknown. I keep saying that fear is a thief and imprisons the mind. And when our mind is bound up, our growth is stunted and it's hard to find the path towards healing. I challenge you today to uncover every mirror in your life. Stop hiding from what you see. Your past mistakes do not define you. The one thing to always keep in mind is that everything you see in those mirrors didn't kill you. You're still here! Don't get tired of your heart words. Speak them until you see your life change. And after it changes, whatever situations you're speaking over, find new heart words that keep affirming your deliverance. You can do this!

CHAPTER 4

DECADES OF WORDS AND SHIFTING

Decade-Shift-Decade:

I NOW REALIZE THAT THERE were patterns and sequences to the events in my life. I was born in 1968. So, there are five decades of events that have cultivated my 50 years to the place where I am today. These life events and shifts are the cornerstone to a movement birthed in my spirit in the now. I've lived through five decades. Five is the number of Grace. We are made after God's image and given favor. The number five is so significant. Man has five senses. Five fingers and toes on each hand and foot. After each decade was a shift from one level to another. I'm talking about major life events. The number eight is significant in each decade. 1968, 78, 88, 98, 2008 and 2018. The number eight is the number of new beginnings. Regeneration. It's the end of one era and the beginning of another. A decade is a 10-year span. The number 10 is the number of a completed course of time, a number of divine order. The symbol of harmony. God's unmerited favor took me through five shifts of divine order and new beginnings all to set me up for such a time as this. Now I understand that God allowed every event in my life to happen for a purpose. A Purpose that has now become clear to me. I'm reminded of Esther. Esther was brought to the King of Persia by her cousin Mordecai to become a part of the Kings Harem. The king notices that she is special, so he makes her queen. But there was a purpose that Esther needed to fulfill. Mordecai urged her that she could not keep silent. He said to her, "Yet who knows whether you have come to the Kingdom for such a time as this." Every event in her life unfolds and plays out like a chess game all leading up to the purpose set before her. I look over my five decades and see that same game for such a time as this.

Decade 1

I was born February 9, 1968, after my mother fought through a terminal diagnosis and decided to resist the doctor's advice. She chose not to accept the finality spoken to her and did not abort me. While in my mother's womb, words like, cancer, kill, abort, were spoken about me. But there was a tug of war, because my mother's words declared were – live and miracle! I wish I could've been a fly on the wall to hear the type of faith conversations it took for my mother to refuse to allow the doctor's words to convince her to end my life before it began. This was the origin of The WOW Effect. It was the lab that was used to create an anecdote that would be introduced to the world five decades later. Every life is born with purpose. Mine was under attack even from the womb. But positive words interrupted that assignment.

The first 10 years of my life were cultivating years. Before the first shift, I had come into the knowledge of certain things prematurely. I learned what infidelity was. I learned from my friends in school that my father was having an affair. I also heard the word "divorce" for the first time. Parents never really know how much children notice. It was a pivotal time in history as my grandmother took ill and had to come live with us, and at that turn of events, my father was also moving out. By the end of the first decade of my life, I had learned a lot and it affected me in a way that I hadn't realized. This little girl who spoke to herself and shared her dreams was trying to escape a place of loneliness and uncertainty. I couldn't figure out what was going on around me. And all my siblings were much older and moving out, so I spoke to the one person who was there. I spoke to the girl in the mirror. Even though she didn't' talk back, I imagined she did, and I imagined she was as excited as I was. It put me in a wonderful place. It made me feel like I could do everything I saw in my dreams. It gave me hope. I can remember that feeling like it was yesterday.

I can still see myself learning how to entertain crowds when there was no one in the room. "And here she is ladies and gentlemen." And the crowd goes wild! That would be the little girl on the back porch of the large two-story wood framed house pretending to be on stage performing before thousands. What I didn't realize was what I was doing back then was a version of what I do today called artist development. Standing on my makeshift stage with a brush in my hand as a microphone, I was coaching myself in performance. I would take two tape recorders and use them to create my own demo tapes by using them to stack harmonies on songs I wrote. My mother sacrificed to buy me a piano that I would sometimes play from sunup to sundown. My mother had the melody to Lionel Richie and Diana Ross's hit song Endless Love etched in her memory, as it was the only piece of sheet music I owned. I developed myself as an artist studying everyone's music and learning every note and word I could. Those words spoken in the mirror would soon become my reality. I would say words like "You're gonna sing in the studios you see on television." And words like one day you're gonna sing with people whose names are in lights, and you will be on Johnny Carson." Little did I know, those words carried a lot of weight. Every word I spoke ushered me into the next shift of my life where I would see the fruit of my verbal seeds.

SHIFT

Decade 2

Prodigy! Incredible! Talented! These were wonderful colorful words I was hearing about the gift of music that had become relevant in this decade. But then I was also introduced to a newfound scene. Bullying. With that came the words ugly, gap-toothed, weird. These are the words that become toxic in your mind. When I was being told, "You think you're cute" I would often question myself saying, "But I don't because you say that I'm ugly because I have a gap between my teeth." Kids can be so cruel and teenage years can carve life-long effects into your existence. The one incredible thing I had in my favor was the knowledge of my gift. I knew I had it and I knew it was powerful. AND... I knew just how to use it to change the atmosphere. Just as I did when I was booed in the seventh-grade beauty pageant. Instead of allowing it to shatter my hopes and dreams, I exercised the power to change how everyone else viewed me. I used my talents and my gift of positive affirmations. When you're faced with adversity, fear, and doubt, I Dare You To Declare. Declare your Vision, No Limits, your Joy, your Life, your Dreams, and your Victory. You can have it ALL!

By the second decade of my life, I had learned the power of this incredible gift. I have a relative who was phenomenally successful in the music industry. This is an industry I have dreamed about working in since I was a little girl. When I was about 19 years old, I found out she was going to be in concert near my hometown. I was super excited and was determined to be in the audience. My goal was to speak to her after the show and share my music that I had been working on. I didn't have big studio money. So, I would sell dinners to raise money for just a few hours of studio time. A supportive friend would often go into her own pocket to help. She had a brother-in-law who would send us instrumental tracks. We would get together and write songs and record them. She would even bring in another friend and they would sing background. (Thank you, Kim, and Monie.) We did what we had to do! Shortly after going to my cousin's show, I was invited to move to Miami to live with her. She wanted me to work with her and she also wanted to groom me in the music industry. This was like a dream come true for me. I knew this was going to open many doors for where I was trying to go. I jumped at the opportunity. Little did I know my decision to follow my dreams was going to come along with a hard road ahead. I wasn't prepared. I had to be taught. My cousin took me under her wing and showed me the ropes. She nurtured me and groomed me. This was not an easy season. Following your dreams calls you to a place of discipline and work. It can be discouraging. The seed of doubt will start to creep into your thoughts and cause you to question everything you had been dreaming about. It can also be destructive, causing you to abort everything you've envisioned. I can't stress to you enough how important it is to value your young years and make the right decisions for your future. Most importantly you must be careful and mindful of the words spoken into your spirit as well as the ones that come out of your own mouth. You can abort your mission before you ever get into it.

This part of the journey can be very rocky. The first lesson learned is, you must believe even when everyone else doesn't. You might start out with everyone in the world behind you, but when it boils down to it, they're looking at you and thinking, "She done lost her mind." Your dream only makes total sense to you. It's YOUR dream. When I think back to that time, I was on a destructive path and didn't know it. My days were spent rarely attending classes and working a job going nowhere, while my nights were spent in clubs and partying. My epiphany came in a strange way. I was sitting at a table in a smoky dark club. There was a drink in front of me and I had a cigarette in my hand. I hated the smell of cigarette smoke and didn't even inhale. So why was I sitting my silly self there with one in my hand and puffing and blowing, going through the motions like an idiot? I thought it made me look cool. Boy was I ever so wrong. This was right after I saw my cousin perform. That was a great night. However, I didn't get to talk to her that night because she was sick. My supportive friends decided to take me to where she lived so we could meet with her with the hopes of something great coming out of it. So here I am at a fork in the road. I'm days away from my trip to meet with my cousin. I walk into the bathroom of this smoky club. In retrospect, I wasn't even having fun. I walked into the ladies' restroom. At the entrance was a wall you had to walk around. On the other side of the wall were the sinks and mirrors. I looked up into this large, well-lit mirror. Staring back at me was someone I didn't recognize. She looked at me and said, "What happened to you? Where's the dreamer? You're going to visit someone very soon who can change your life forever! Why are you here? Is this really what you want? If you don't take a different turn now, you will destroy your future." I started to shake. My palms got sweaty. I was so afraid. Imagine me looking around to see if anyone else in the bathroom could hear what this person in the mirror was saying to me. I knew at that moment, things HAD to change. When you reach a place where there's a paradigm shift in your life, you will either shift or miss the moment. That encounter was a warning sign. Have you ever been traveling and saw a road sign that reads, "Last Exit Before Tolls"? Well, this was my last exit before destruction. I had to exit. The Bible says God will always give you a way of escape." Who knows what could have happened if I hadn't taken heed to the words spoken to me in my spirit? WOW! A few days later I was in the car with my friends on the road trip to meet with my cousin. This trip was exactly what I believed it would be. Life changing. As I told you I was invited to live with her, and she taught me some critical things. But I will never forget something she said to me that very day. She said, "You have a humbling voice. You must be careful what comes out of your mouth." Now at the time, I thought it was all about singing. Little did I know that those words would come back to me 30 years later and have an impact as if she had set a time bomb to explode. I like to call these words "Heart Words" These are words expressed from an inward place based on what you know, practice and have experienced. My cousin, Betty Wright transitioned to be with the Lord in 2020. She was a God fearing, bible reading, God serving woman who lived a life of faith. She never allowed fame and fortune to compromise her relationship with God. She spoke what God had her to say to me prophetically in that very moment. Heart Words! When your heart and mind is filled with good things, motivational and inspiring truths, good words will come out of your mouth. But there is also other stuff like negativity, strife, doom, and gloom. Heart words. Kinda makes you go, hmmmmmm. Heart words can fertilize and water a beautifully planted seed. And Heart words can turn right back around, and spray weed killer on its first blossom. Here I am, launched into a great career. Heart words can also be those words in your spirit that God speaks to you giving you warning signs and reminded comfort.

My cousin took me everywhere she went. Placed me on the microphone in almost every session she booked. And one day she took me into a session that changed everything. She was a good friend of Gloria Estefan. Gloria had recently been in an unbelievably bad accident where she was slammed into a table on her tour bus and broke her back. Miraculously, a surgeon saved her from being paralyzed. She started working on an album about her experience. My cousin was her vocal coach, vocal producer, and arranger for the project. I was one of those chosen for an opportunity to sing on those records. It was an experience that elevated me, and my worth as a singer. It was also an exciting time. We spent weeks with the Estefans. We got to know the whole family and all the band members. We would often have lunch with them and engage in conversations about plans for upcoming tours, family, and all sorts of topics. The gift or two Dalmatian puppies that were recently given to Gloria after her accident would also often be one of the hot topics in the break room. It's one of those experiences you hate to see end.

Although this was the chance of a lifetime, it was still a tough season. Work was sometimes scarce. Gigs can sometimes be few and far in between. It's normal for a singer or actor to have many small jobs between gigs. Well not long after the Gloria Estefan sessions, I was working one of those jobs at a pizza restaurant. My job was to be by the phone and write down pizza orders and prepare deliveries. Hey, it gave me a paycheck. Months had gone by since those recording sessions at the Estefan's studio. I'm sure the project was being completed, mixed, and mastered. It usually takes six months to a year for an album to be ready for release. All I had at that point was great memories. So, I thought.

Here I am between music gigs, with my head down making sure I have the order information correct, when suddenly I hear this familiar voice. I hear that voice call my name, "Anita?" I looked up and there was my 11th grade English teacher. "Oh wow! Hi" I said. We started having thy typical "What are you doing?" conversation. We talked about college and me working with my cousin in the exciting music industry. And suddenly a memory sparked. A conversation I had with Emilio at one of those famous lunches in the break room surfaced. On the last day of recording, Emilio mentioned that Gloria was considering for the first-time taking background singers on tour with her. He asked if I would be interested. Of course, my response was "Yes!" This thought entered my mind in that very conversation I was having with my 11th grade English teacher. I thought to myself, how did I miss this? Immediately I started to speak to her about the music I had been recording with Gloria Estefan. I said to her "and I will be going on tour with her in the future" There it was. I began to speak life over the conversation I had with Emilio. I didn't know when, but I knew that it was on the mind of Gloria and Emilio because they mentioned it to me. I also knew that this was what I wanted. So, I started making plans to prepare for it. This was a gift in me that I didn't realize I had. It had been with me my entire life. That same little imaginative girl who was talking to herself was now 19-20 years old and at a pivotal time in my life. Heart words were coming out of my mouth. I talked about it so much, people were tired of me. My family was like, "yea yea we hear you." Now don't get me wrong, they loved me and wanted the best for me, but it was hard for them to see it. It wasn't their vision. It was mine! Well, many weeks passed. And one day I got that phone call. WOW! I was going on tour with Gloria Estefan and the Miami Sound Machine. A dream comes true! I was over the top excited. I traveled all over the world. I saw more than I even imagined in my dreams. I traveled to Italy, London, Paris, Spain, Colombia, Brazil, Japan, Australia...... You name it! I went there. Two years later, I was in a shopping mall in my hometown. I was standing at a jewelry counter. My head was down admiring something under the glass. I hear this familiar voice say, "Anita?" I looked up and there was my 11th grade English teacher. "Oh, my goodness!" she screamed. She started speaking with so much pride and excitement. She said, "I remember the day I ran into you, and you told me you would be touring with Gloria Estefan. So, from that day, every time I heard anything mentioned about her, I was all eyes and ears. And finally, one day I looked up at my television and there you were. My student singing and performing with Gloria Estefan." There it was. The effects of the W.O.W. manifested., I was happy that I listened to my heart. The words were there. They came to life when I spoke to them with certainty. I didn't speak gloom and doom. No matter what people around me thought, I would continue to speak life. This is what I want you to understand about whatever is in your heart. Affirmation begins with you. You must be the one to speak life before anyone else. Your dream is about to burst inside you. Some people have been pregnant with purpose so long that they are overdue. Is that you? When you learn how to use your words, life will be forever changed. You have the power to turn any situation around. You have the power to speak your dreams to life. You have the power to change your situation today. The words are in your heart. SPEAK THEM!

This decade also came with multiple significant deaths that were extremely hard. Not only for me, but more so for my mother. She buried several siblings and her mother (my grandmother). There was so much in the turn of this decade, I don't know where to begin. My parents were not educated people. They were hard workers who did their best with what they had. Regardless of what my mother didn't experience, she still drove me to become educated but had no idea how to help me achieve it nor could she afford it. I had to figure things out for myself. I graduated from high school and was preparing for college. With that transition comes the "I'm grown" disease. Boy did this cost me. This disease cost me time, opportunities, relationships, respect; you name it. I was so determined to be my own boss, that I didn't' realize I was falling prey to the tricks of the devil who wanted to cause me to forfeit my destiny. I made so many poor decisions. Toxic Word Syndrome was in full effect. It was causing me to have a cloudy thought life. I heard what I wanted to hear. If a man said, "You fine mama," I heard "I love you." This type of behavior caused me to enter relationships, whether personal or friendship or business, which were toxic and unproductive. If only girls would learn in this transition in life that Mama really does know best.

I was raised a church girl all my life. Although my thoughts looking back on those days remind me of the strict doctrine we were subjected to, the foundational value of my upbringing was extremely valuable. So, in my adulthood, I went back to my roots and desired to live the Christian life I was taught. Little did I know, there was a great challenge awaiting me. I experienced my first bout with "church hurt". So many people are victimized by institutionalized hypocrisy and scandal that sometimes come out in those who start off with the best of intentions. Church hurt is so devastating because of the trust one has in the members and leaders. It's often some of the most toxic relationships we enter. These relationships are often out of the will of God and can in some cases be a form of idolatry. We don't' realize it at the time but we become infected by a generational church membership programming of the mind. And because we are indoctrinated in a system of practices, we don't develop a relationship with God, we develop a devout bond to the church system. I found myself right here in this decade. The system had me. And once you get caught up in this, your judgment is cloudy. I found myself in a Tsunami of toxic thoughts, which produced toxic words that led to poor choices. This led to a ferocious wave of false accusations and public scrutiny. It's awfully hard to stand through gossip and lies. I learned a hard lesson about trying to defend myself verbally. In cases like this, silence is golden. If I would've known what to do, or better yet what NOT to do, I could've saved myself a lot of heartache. I could've put a whole new spin on "Stand still and see the salvation of the Lord." But during the shift I was going into a situation that would elevate me to a better place. Going into this shift had me feeling like I was escaping a prison of pain and misery. And then I shifted.

S H I F T

Decade 3

This is a decade that held some of the most wonderful experiences of my life as well as some of the most difficult ones. It started off with a BANG! So, I thought. I was escaping a prison and coming into the birthing of a career I had been dreaming about since childhood. I was shifting from the ending of a decade being called a Floozy and a loser, into a decade being called humbling and promising. At the turn of this completed course of time, I was entering a season of remarkable success. My career had taken a leap and I was about to be traveling all over the world. I had met and married a man that I thought I would spend my life with. Shortly after my fairytale wedding, I started traveling in a way I had never experienced before. My travel started in Yokohama, Japan. So, imagine me having barely been out of the state of Florida, then suddenly, I'm going to countries I couldn't pronounce. It was an amazing experience. This decade is where Toxic Word Syndrome was no longer like a dormant disease. It now became FULL BLOWN!

I got married to a man I loved more than life, at the brink of a career shift that changed my life forever. Young marriages are difficult. Communication is often muddied because of lack of maturity or plain old adjustments and growing pains. Without thought, the language between lovers can become very colorful, for lack of a better phrase. I know some people who would argue that being cursed out and called a bitch and every other name in the book is not verbal abuse. I beg to differ. There's an act of manipulation there. When you're subjected to verbal slurs daily, it doesn't feel good. It makes you sad and it hurts to hear someone you love speak to you this way. So, you find yourself putting up with anything and making compromises just to keep peace. This is not healthy. You allow yourself to absorb all this negativity. You allow yourself to become a verbal dartboard and each word sticks you like a sharp dart. That pain and discomfort doesn't just go away. NO. Think about it. You can sense it. So, your thoughts go back to what was said to you in yesterday's fight. And God knows you don't wanna go back there. So, you go into prevention mode. There you are, reliving it. There's the tape recorder on repeat playing it repeatedly. TWS was in full effect.

After five years of marriage, it ended in separation and then a few years later, divorce. Divorce is devastating. It's like a death. You lose a part of you. It tears you in half, and with the absence of the other half you must regenerate and heal. In my healing process I joined a local ministry. In the beginning it was amazing. Everything I needed at the time was within my reach. I had even accepted a calling into ministry during this decade. Funny how when the pastor asked me what I felt would be my biggest struggle as a person walking this walk of faith, my response was "public scrutiny." Go figure! And yet again, I found myself in yet another war against the mouths of others. Why can't people just keep their words off me?!! Through this process, not only did I put a lesson I had learned in the earlier decade to effective use, but I also learned one of the most valuable lessons of my life. You must be careful how you respond to toxic words coming at you. Here I was again being victimized by the toxic words of people. How could this be happening again? Along with it came isolation and humiliation. The lesson from the earlier decade that I learned was not to try to respond or tell my side of the story. It only fuels the fire. Some battles you leave for God while you stand boldly and quietly. The words did affect me. I found myself using my little girl tactic, talking to myself, and affirming myself, to stay sane, while being isolated and publicly humiliated.

At the culmination of this decade, my family chain was broken for the first time. I experienced the first death of any descendants of my parents. I held the hand of my nine-year-old, great nephew as he left this earth from Leukemia. It was a devastating blow. No matter how much I spoke life, it was God's will for him to go. There was a need for a shift out of this decade. I had attended a conference where I received a word of prophecy that said, "Before 1998 you will see the victory." And sure enough, before the end of that year, I knew what was in store for me. I knew where I was going and when I was leaving. I knew I needed a profound change! So, I Shifted.

S H I F T

Decade 4

They that wait upon the Lord shall renew their strength. They will mount up on wings as eagles. They will run and not be weary. They will walk and not faint. Isaiah 40:31 was my anthem. I felt so good about this shift. The words that come to mind are renewed and rescued. This is exactly what it felt like. I was offered a new job in a new city. A pastor of a mega ministry seized the opportunity to have me come and work in his church. It was like he swept in and rescued a damsel in distress and made the boogie man go away. I had been rescued from smugglers holding me for ransom. It was liberating. But what I didn't realize was, to whom much is given, much is required. Wow did this take on a whole new meaning. I took on a huge responsibility, which meant more people. More people meant a whole new level of potential TWS. Man! Is there a vaccine for this condition? Wouldn't that be great? My new shift led to more work. So much that the workload was meant for 10 people. And it wasn't long before I realized I had entered an epidemic of TWS. It was everywhere I turned. I couldn't escape it. It was on a level that I could never have imagined. There's one thing I noticed that was different. In the other decades, each time I was subjected to TWS, the exposure was three to five years. But in this situation, I was exposed for the entire 10 years. I felt like I was in a TWS prison, and I couldn't get out.

I had started a business on the side and was proud to be working on something that really spoke the essence of who I am. Music! I felt alive again for the first time in years! A young man I hired as a musician recognized the gift I had for writing, arranging, and producing music. The friendship and business relationship that developed brought the gift inside me back to life. I'm forever grateful to my friend Ron for helping restore that part of me. I know it had to be the dormant gift inside along with positive words spoken about the work I was doing that gave me so much life. It was liberating to know that something I created was making the lives of others better. I was helping dreams come true. That has meaning. It's fulfilling. WOW! My work was just getting off the ground. And in one conversation, toxic words attacked it. Something that starts out so pure and innocent, can suddenly become dark and desolate when poison is spewed over it. Imagine having a beautiful garden full of the most beautiful roses. Roses that are rare and some of which most eyes have never seen. People would come from all over the world just to lay eyes on its rare beauty. This garden planted by you and nurtured by you is breath taking. Even you have a tough time believing you created it. Then suddenly, someone comes through with a dangerous weed killer, who doesn't distinguish weeds from good flora, and sprays it all over your garden. This is what happened to me and that beautiful business I created. When you're working in a hostile, toxic environment, it's only a matter of time before your good will be spoken evil of. That's the danger of toxicity. It spreads everywhere. The thought of it makes me quiver. My business was called a curse. The toxicity was so overwhelming that all my hard work started to suffocate. Isn't that something? Like weeds in your rose garden just taking over. Sucking the life out of your productivity. The words – Greedy. Untrustworthy. Thief. Cursed (everything about me, my business and everyone who does business with me) This is where I had to make my exit. Enough was enough. I had to get myself into a place where there was no TWS. Why did I end up here again? I made a mad dash out! And just like that, I shifted.

S H I F T

Decade 5

Quarantine. This is where I ended up. The only way I could protect myself was to go into quarantine. When you're placed into quarantine, it's a place of protection and isolation for if you had been exposed to and infectious, contagious disease. And to keep it from spreading or affecting others, you must be quarantined. This was a wonderful place for me. I spent three WHOLE years in quarantine. I wanted to make sure I was cleared of the effects of TWS. One of the things I did to pass time was send out short audio devotionals once a week just to encourage people. I would always end with 'WOW... Be Blessed and Be Free". It wasn't scripted. It was how I felt. I started to realize the power of words. I only wanted to share how good words helped me with others. I wanted them to experience the amount of encouragement that positive words could give.

This decade was also very eye opening. At the turn of this decade, I suffered the loss of a sibling. My brother passed away. It was a tough period to watch my mother feel the pain of burying her child. Three months later I lost two close friends within a month of each other. And then later that following year, my father passed away. These events taught me how short life really was. I'd heard people say that all my life, but at this point, I got it! But even through the series of losses I was able to keep my sanity and my peace with a little dose of W.O.W.

It was the most peaceful time I'd had ever. I spent most of this decade building businesses and networking. Some situations worked well, and some were downright awful. But in this decade, I was good on words. I had started to get what The W.O.W Effect was doing. There's something that I've noticed. The toxic words may still be around, but I feel like my immune system fights them and wards them off much better. WOW!! It's the W.O.W Effect. It has become a part of my everyday regimen. I started really living and not existing. But I heard Bishop Victor T Curry say, "No one is immune to storms. You're either on your way into one, currently in one, or just coming out of one." Five years into this decade my stormy season came when my mother had a cardiac arrest. I remember the night I got the call that she needed CPR and had to be revived by a defibrillator. I uttered these words, "Lord please don't take her now. I'm not ready." God heard my prayer, and it was His will for me to have her a little longer. I brought her to live with me during her golden years. It was a tough period for my family and me, but we were able to survive. Thank God for The W.O.W Effect.

As I told you, No one is immune to storms. Five years later, Mom made her transition. For those who have lost a mother, you understand what I mean when I say you feel lost. Your main cheerleader, your ride or die, your greatest support is no longer living and breathing on this earth. It was a hard pill to swallow. When you experience this sense of emptiness, it leaves you questioning everything. And then......

SHIFT

I'm turning 50. I look up and realize there must be MORE than this. I'm missing something. What is it? W.O.W! That's what it is. The scales have now fallen off my eyes. Five decades in, I'm realizing one of the most wonderful things about my existence. There were five decades. My name has five letters. ANITA. It means "God is gracious" five is also the number of grace. Every time my name is spoken, I'm having that phrase spoke to me. You've survived so much Anita. Why? Well, it's all said in my name. God is gracious. W.O.W talk about Words Optimizing Wholeness!

This is it, huh? I saw the paradigm shift in my life. And this is the BIG one as people say. My entire life has been designed for this very moment. How amazing is that? It became as clear as a crystal glass to me. My purpose revealed. I must share with the world that Words Optimize Wholeness. No matter what your situation is, you have the power of life and death in your tongue. We just need to learn to watch our mouths. And we also must learn how to block and filter our hearing. The W.O.W Effect will change your life.

QUARANTINE IS NOT SUCH A BAD WORD

Quarantine

*W*HEN I WENT INTO quarantine, I wanted to completely distance myself from anything potentially harmful to me. I wanted absolutely no parts of toxic activity. After spending 2 decades of my adult life in toxicity, it was time to go into isolation and deal with the issues. It was rock bottom. And I was starting over. I had to lay the target to rest. It was time to make some changes and stop taping and gluing the shattered pieces together. I had to stop pulling the weeds back just enough to breathe. This was not how life was supposed to be for me. I was not designed to just lay down and take it. I'm supposed to be a victor not a victim. Instead of pulling those weeds back from around your one little lonely blossom, it's time to tend to the garden and get rid of the weeds that are taking up space and blocking nutrition and sunlight.

Uproot the weeds

A weed is a plant that is not valued where it is growing, and it usually grows vigorously. They tend to overgrow or choke out the good plants. Toxic words do the same thing in your mind. No matter how much you hear someone tell you how great you are and how beautiful you are, if your mind is full of toxic negative thoughts about yourself, you will never be able to receive the benefits of good words. Your mind has become so crowded from the bad stuff, and now those words are on replay and are echoing in your thoughts. No wonder there's no productivity. To get rid of this pattern, you must get down to the origin. First you must acknowledge that the words are there. This is a tough phase because it causes you to confront the pain. Some things in your life were so devastating that you have chosen to block it out. To uproot it, call it out. Identify it. Otherwise, they will continue to regenerate fear, doubt, failure, defeat, and brokenness. Remember weeds don't need help. They regenerate themselves. You must dig deep within your soul and expose all the negative things that have plagued you from moving forward in your purpose. Identify all the negative statements that have been hindering your progress. This is an ugly revelation. But the good thing to remember is that you're exposing them to get rid of them. And once you go through the process, you will have to destroy them.

Once you have named the weeds, you must get down in the dirt to pull them up by the root. Some of these roots have been inside you for many years. Maybe even all your life. You must dig deep around them and pull them up and be careful not to break the root off. You don't want to give it a chance to regrow. When a farmer is trying to pull up a weed from dry soil, or with one that has stubborn roots, sometimes they will take some boiling water and pour it on the weed to kill it and loosen the soil. This is how aggressive we must be for those stubborn weeds that have been with you since childhood. The bullying words that replay. If a little girl is being told, "you're ugly" by bullies, those words will take root and grow and continue to replay in her mind until she believes it. Then years later in her adult life, if she's in a verbally abusive relationship or marriage, and the same words come out of the mouth of the abuser; it will cause the pain from the little girl to resurface. And there it is. They start to regenerate even more and even stronger. Those weeds need to be killed and uprooted. I told you this wasn't easy. It hurts. It may leave gaping holes in your heart. But the root must go. Also, there are some weeds that must be salted. This will ensure that the weeds never return. The bible mentions many different uses for salt. Salt was used to season food. It was used as a preservative. Salt was also used to cleanse newborns and prevent infection, and to heal diseases of the skin. And when there was land to be conquered, they would pour salt on the ground so that nothing could grow there again. This is the approach we must take to the weeds in our mental garden. There are a few patches that need to be salted. There are a few areas that are so invaded that you need to salt it so that it never has the possibility of regenerating again.

Can you imagine what the ground would look like after all the pulling, scouring, and digging? I'm sure it wouldn't look like there was ever a garden there before. I'm sure it would be torn to shreds with holes in the ground and debris everywhere.

When you're working to replant your mental garden, pull the weeds up, and then lay them out in the sun to let them dry out and die. In some cases, once they've completely dried out people would opt to burn them. We name them, we kill them and uproot them, we lay them out to dry and then we burn them. Now I'm sure that when you think about this process in the natural it seems harsh. What you must remember is that we have been storing up words that served no purpose but to destroy us. Why would you want to preserve or hold onto anything that smothers you? Why stay in a situation that doesn't allow you to breathe and grow and be fruitful? We have all been guilty of hurting ourselves at some point or another. But now you can start over. Weeds are up and burned and the soil is ready for preparation

When I hit my rock bottom and went into what I call quarantine, it took me about three years to deal with the weeds in my garden. I was carrying stuff that had been growing since birth. Not only was I in quarantine, but I was also in isolation. I had been broken for so long, that the illness was starting to contaminate not only me, but the people around me. The negativity was so intense it started to rub off onto others. I was unknowingly and unintentionally spewing my toxins over other people's hopes and dreams. I was sick and I needed help. Isolation separates sick people with a contagious disease from people who are not sick. Quarantine separates and restricts the movement of people who were exposed to a contagious disease to see if they become sick. So not only did I isolate myself to keep others from becoming contaminated by my toxins, but I also Quarantined myself so I wouldn't be exposed to any more toxic words than I already was as well as to assure myself that the disease wouldn't return. In this place I had to look at the torn-up garden and determine that there was hope. This is where I had to pick up the rake and till the soil. Tilling the soil is a process that should be well thought out and carefully done. Not only are you raking up the leftover debris, but also you must be careful not to disturb the good stuff. There are beneficial earthworms and humus and organic matter from the leaf tillage and the decayed animals that make the soil more fertile. When I was in this place in my life, I had to take the time to delicately till the soil in my spirit. The soil was dry and malnourished. It lacked luster and nutrients and moisture. All the right components need to be in the soil before it can be conditioned for seeds to germinate. After tilling the ground, we have to fertilize. Jesus said that we are the salt of the earth. Different from the salt I was referring to earlier that preserves. But this metaphor was referring to us being the fertilizer of the earth. Fertilizer adds nitrogen, phosphorus, and nutrients to the soil. This makes the ground conducive for growth and promotes a healthy harvest. I was in a season of preparation.

My quarantine season was one of the most peaceful times of my life. I was in my own little world where I controlled the climate and traffic. This was the only way I could properly treat my soil. I needed time, silence, and space. There was so much that took place in this season, and I now believe that if I weren't in quarantine, I wouldn't have been able to focus on taking care of my mother. God always knows when things need to be removed from your life and when you need to be removed from people and places. I had a great foundation. My mother raised me well with a lot of love and direction. She instilled the love of God in me. This encouraged me as my soil was prepared for the next phase of my life. No matter what, I knew that I was working with high quality, fertile ground.

Planting Season

Now it was time. It was time for me to make some drastic changes. I found myself in that place where I talked to myself. I always knew that if nobody else heard me, believed in me, and loved me, God did. Now you may want to ask me "If you were so aware of God's love for you, then how did you ever get so low?" You must always remember that you are not immune to storms and trials. But it's how equipped you are for the storms that will determine your condition after the storm. If you're not equipped with the necessary supplies, you could suffer damage and destruction. So, as many times as I found myself exposed to TWS, I was not properly equipped for the words. My mind was not guarded. I was exposed and vulnerable to the toxins. My spiritual immune system was weak. And then after the storm hit, I failed to do proper clean up because I lacked the proper tools. There was debris still around and damages unrepaired. Therefore, leaving me susceptible to destruction that got worse and worse as another storm hit and then another and another. After there was nothing left to destroy, I decided to regenerate my garden. After everything was pulled up, and the soil was tilled and the fertilizer was down, I knew what was next. I knew it was time to plant. I'm talking about planting good seeds into good soil. There's nothing more liberating than knowing what you can expect to grow in your garden. For every negative word that I uprooted, I felt like I needed to plant multiple positive words. But before I took a step in that direction, I decided to just spend some time treating the soil. Sometimes you must wait a while to see if there are any weeds straggling behind. You have to see if there are any seeds or roots that went unnoticed. Every now and then I would catch some weeds trying to resurface. The phone would ring, or I would get some hearsay. So, I had to get my scalding hot water and salt and go to work. No MORE WEEDS HERE! I sat still in isolation and quarantine for a long time. Several years in fact. It was the most peaceful time of my life. Finally, my mind was still.

I prayed and worshipped. I could hear God again. When your thoughts are toxic and you have negativity floating around in your spirit, you can't hear God. So, at this point I was overjoyed that I got my joy and my peace back. I spent a lot of time meditating on one of my favorite passages of scripture.

Philippians 4:6-8 *"Be careful for nothing; but in everything by prayer and supplication with thanksgiving let your requests be made known unto God. And the peace of God, which passeth all understanding, shall keep your hearts and minds through Christ Jesus. Finally, brethren, whatsoever things are true, whatsoever things are honest, whatsoever things are just, whatsoever things are pure, whatsoever things are lovely, whatsoever things are of good report; if there be any virtue, and if there be any praise, think on these things."*

This entire time was my time of release and healing. I could never move forward from all the pain and toxins if I didn't take the time to deal with the issues head on. Sometimes we make the awful mistake of sweeping our pain under a rug to hide it from people. We become so accustomed to that that we don't even realize that we're trying to hide it from ourselves. I was so happy for the new, found peace. I was able to dream again. I had hope again. I knew I could NEVER go back to that place. I was willing to do whatever I needed to prepare myself for anything else to come. I thought I was prepared before. No, it was just tape and glue. So out went the tape and glue along with the target and the vase. No longer would my mind be invaded. I have good soil. I'm planting goods seeds. This was certainly a new beginning.

LET IT GROW

$\mathcal{N}$OTHING MAKES A FARMER prouder than to step out into the midst of the field and see the fruits of their labor. After going through the agricultural process of preparation, sowing, fertilizing, and irrigation, he must then prepare for harvesting. After going through so much in my thirties, I was determined that my forties would be different. And they were. I didn't escape the changes that came along with life, but I was not subjected to the toxicity that had plagued me for years. It's extremely challenging to try again after a bad harvest. But you must. It makes no sense to have that beautiful field called a mind and not use it. You can live up to your fullest potential.

A bad harvest can leave a sour taste in your mouth. I remember saying: "I never want to know this kind of pain ever again." I was so adamant that I tried everything in my power not to put myself in the position of ever being subjected to anything that could ever cause me to be exposed to TWS. Wishful thinking. You will always be exposed, but you need to be covered to temper the exposure. Don't allow yourself to think you can live in a bubble. I was close to making that mistake. I spent a year closing myself off from the world and people. Going through traumatic experiences can leave you with one of the most traumatic battle wounds ever - Failure! After a bad harvest, there's usually a shortage of whatever you're growing. After uprooting all the toxic words and turning the soil, my spirit was drained. I had gone through the process of forgiving others who hurt me, but there was one person I did not forgive. That person was me.

Going through emotional trauma, public scrutiny and heartbreak can make you reluctant to even try anything again. The emptiness and lonely season that follows causes your emotions to tell you the lie that you are a failure. Remember, failure is an event. It's not who you are. The toughest part after a bad harvest is sowing and tending to the crop not knowing if it's going to be successful. We can't allow the event of failure to cause us to not produce. Back in the day, if you didn't sow and tend to your crops, you didn't eat. If we don't replenish the fields of our minds with new words and positive thoughts, we won't produce. Visions and dreams will die. It's like falling off a horse. They say the best thing to do is to get back up and conquer the fear of falling again. I know, it's easier said than done.

So many times in my life, I have had to face the music of starting over. Remember that young girl in the seventh grade who was booed on stage? Yes, that was me. After that experience, it was tough to sign up for the next pageant. Even when you do your best to forget traumatic experiences, sometimes there's a peanut gallery around you who won't let you forget. There I was, only two years past the still fresh wounds of embarrassment, signing up for yet another pageant. Don't get me wrong; I had closed the mouths of everyone that booed me when I sang the roof off the gymnasium during the talent segment. But there was still an unsettledness in my nerves that I couldn't ignore. That coupled with the reminder from the gallery:" Girl! You brave! Remember when you got booed off the stage?" It sure didn't help defuse the fear bomb inside me that was about to have me withdraw from the competition.

I don't think I have ever shared this story with anyone. But I know the very moment that I felt like I could manifest my dreams of working in the music industry and singing all over the world. That moment came about because of my ninth-grade school beauty pageant. Shell shocked and all, there I was again about to brush off the dirt and get back on the horse. I don't think I had ever been so nervous. The same boy that I had rejected was also zoned for this school as well. The audition results were in, and I was about to find out if I would be a contestant. When the list was posted everybody ran towards the chorus room door to see whose names made the list. I can still remember how fast my heart was beating. I wasn't nervous about whether my name would be on the list. I knew it would for the most part. My uneasiness was about hitting the stage again and being booed. No matter how much I practiced my talent routine, my evening gown walks and my interview questions, I still had this huge lump in the back of my throat. Nobody likes to revisit traumatic experiences. I had no idea how everyone would react. I was hopeful that those who knew me from seventh grade would remember. I would practice at home in the mirror, telling myself, "Girl! You are gonna bring the house DOWN!" I put my old faithful mirror conversations to use.

The time came for the moment of truth. I started singing the song "Out Here on My Own", sung by Irene Cara in the movie *FAME*. My church girl instincts always managed to kick in with the soulful riffs and runs. As I slowly started to sing, you could hear the gasps from the audience. As my voice gripped the melody and started to rev up with intensity, the audience erupted with outbursts of applause. That was new. My nerves got less and less jittery. Then when I hit the climax of the song, they started screaming and shouting and ended in a standing ovation. WOW! I was convinced. I knew from that moment that my life was special, and I had a serious gift. The kind of gift that changes and impacts lives.

I knew it! I knew my affirmations worked. If I wanted something to happen or a certain outcome, I would just start talking about it. I had to change the climate. I spent two years preparing for that one moment. I had my eyes on that ninth-grade pageant right after the seventh grade one. I took my time, chose the right song and the right evening gown. But the most important piece of the puzzle was reprogramming my mind so that I could do it. In the seventh-grade pageant, I was able to make it through the performance and perform well despite the boos. And I was able to make it past the chatter in the weeks and months that followed.

I've shared with you that I have always battled with rejection and public scrutiny. I was rejected in the womb. As a child, I felt the spirit of rejection when my father abandoned his family by having an affair, which led to divorce. I've dealt with rejection and public scrutiny in school, church and in the community. After each dramatic episode in my life that played out like a syndicated television program, I was able to get back on the horse again. But when you have never dealt with the seeds sown into your mental garden, you will reap a harvest so bad that you will need to destroy it and start over. This is where I was at the time I referred to as quarantine.

Applying The W.O.W Effect saved my life. I served every negative thought, phrase and word that had ever been planted in my subconscious an eviction notice. I went back as far as I could remember, and even passed that to what preceded my memory but was shared with me. Yes, I went back to the doctor who gave my mom that false diagnosis when she was pregnant with me. I went to every conversation that I overheard that I wasn't supposed to hear. Every adult who insulted my existence, every child who didn't understand what made me so special, and every non-relationship relationship, which poisoned my mind about myself, were all served eviction notices. After evicting all the madness, treating the soil, planting new words and watering my crop, I was able to sit back and admire the growth. It's as freeing and as peaceful as watching a farmer sit on the porch looking out at the endless view of a beautiful new budding harvest. The more you nurture it, and the more you water it, the more it grows. Once I uprooted the bad crop, I burned it, treated my soil, and then I planted good seeds. I got rid of the toxic words and planted new and positive words. Then I entered the growth stage. This is a very delicate and interesting process. Humans go through progressions of growth – infant, toddler, adolescent, young adult, adult, and elderly. Well, I look at mind transformation the same way. The human growth progressions are much like that of plants – sprout, seeding, vegetative, budding, flowering, and ripening. The mind goes through stages of progression just like that as well.

After treating the soil and getting it to a productive state, you plant. This is what I had to do to my mind. Once the good words were planted and nurtured, the stages of my growth and healing began to take place. If you've ever planted a garden in your own yard, you know the feeling you get when you see that first ray of hope. That's the sprouting phase. That's when the seed germinates and starts to grow its first set of leaves. This shows that there is life. Wh®en you have truly created a change in your mindset, you'll start noticing that your language will change. *"For out of the abundance of the heart, the mouth speaks" – Matthew 12:34.* Instead of coming out negative, life starts to flow. This is as good as the feeling when you see your garden sprouting. You start smiling and talking to the sprout like it's a newborn baby. It's a great feeling. That WOW Effect is doing its job. It makes you excitedly anticipate what's next. Although the sprouts are there, they're still delicate so you must handle them with care. Because the next phase is what causes the seed you planted to stick. This is the seedling phase

Seedling is when the roots develop and spread. The roots absorb nutrients so the plant can become healthy. The healthier the roots are, the healthier the plant is. This process is where you take your sprouts and plant them in a larger pot so the roots can continue to grow. At this state, it's important to give abundant care to the plant. You must make sure it has adequate sunlight and daily watering. This lesson was hard to learn. Just because I had cleared my bad harvest and started planting new seeds, didn't mean I could relax. This is where the work comes in. I didn't realize how vulnerable I was until I saw some personal sprouts die from lack of care. I didn't realize that it wasn't just about water and sunlight, but I also had to protect them from harsh rains and debris that could easily upset the rooting and growth process.

When I first started walking in my new emotional and mental place, I was content with a few words of positivity. I was proudly showing off my sprouts. This was new growth. And then BOOM! Here came negativity. Not AGAIN!!! I thought I got rid of you. Beware, negativity can invade your new garden of thought like a hurricane. Therefore, the Bible says to "guard your heart and mind." You have a responsibility to your sprouts to protect and nurture them. Because there's more growing to be done.

Once the roots have grown and the plant is visibly showing growth, the vegetative phase starts. This is where photosynthesis takes place. It's when the plant turns light into its own chemical energy. Light is essential. If you picked up this book, then you were probably where I was at my lowest point in my life. If I didn't have faith, I don't know where I would have ended up. In the darkest moments is where remarkable things can be birthed. In a dark place is where seeds take root. You can't see what's happening, but you know it is because you have faith in the seed you planted. Just like the plants need light in the vegetative state, so do we. My prayer life and meditation were the light I needed to keep my new harvest growing. This is the most important phase for daily affirmations. You need to continuously put good words and good thoughts into your mind and speak them aloud. It's like you're echoing what's on the inside of you. And as you echo your thoughts, you reaffirm what God has already said to you privately. And just watch the growth in your life begin to happen.

There's another phase that plants evolve into - the budding phase. It's a reproductive cycle that allows the plant to grow more buds. And this is relevant to the positivity in your thinking. That positive light starts to spread over every area of your life. Just like a plant that starts out cute and tiny, and then suddenly it starts to take over the pot it's in. I remember planting basil. I was amazed at how a tiny seed could produce so much basil that I couldn't use in time. I had so much I was able to share it. This is what positive energy does. You can walk into a room and your presence could cut the tension with a knife. When you are budding with positive thoughts and words, you can become unstoppable. Therefore, stay on that daily dose of The WOW Effect.

Where there are buds, there's fruit. The next phase is the flowering phase. This is a sweet phase. This is the transporting of sugars and starches to produce flowers and fruit. When positive words are in your mind, positive statements come out of your mouth. When positive statements come out of your mouth, your life will become fruitful. When we think better, we speak better. When we speak better, we live better. This is what you've been working for Mr. & Ms. Farmer. All the demanding work from uprooting the bad harvest to now is what allows you to partake of the next phase, which is ripening. When fruit is ripening, it goes through a process called flushing. About six weeks before harvest, flushing takes place. Flushing is when you flush out the excess salts, nutrients and contaminates. Just like with plants, farmers will use nutrients and fertilizers to help the crops and protect them. Sometimes in life we use resources and materials and artificial comforts to protect our thoughts or our mental crops. But when you flush the harvest, you give it only water.

We must turn our plates down and fast sometimes to flush out the impurities and toxins, so our fruit won't be contaminated. What's so great about this is that you can harvest your fruit in the best state it could be in. My life started to take the best turn ever when I reconnected to my faith and allowed God to flush out anything that would cause me to even think I was still where I use to be. It can be a little scary for farmers to start picking the harvest, especially when it's being rushed or if you are not sure about it. That's why you must go through the process, I guarantee you that if you follow the instructions, your fruit will be plentiful and sweet. God is faithful! The WOW Effect works. When you can stand back and admire your crop, you can sigh and say to yourself "This is what freedom feels like."

CHAPTER

BE BLESSED AND BE FREE

*H*APPY BIRTHDAY TO ME. Happy Birthday to me. Happy Birthday dear Anita (God is Gracious) Happy Birthday to me. February 9, 2018. My 50th birthday. Here I am Fifty, Fabulous and FREE! Now what? This is where I found myself after having completed the latest decade of my life. I was entering yet another year with the significance of the number eight and another shift. But there was such a difference from this shift and all the others shifts in my life. This past decade was all about replanting the garden in my mind. This decade was full of adjustments and changes. There were also some significant, life altering, events in this decade. But the main thing was that I had walked into the greatest sense of freedom of my entire life. For the first time I didn't have the cloudy thoughts. For the first time I was walking in the newness of a fresh weed free harvest in my mind. This was certainly new for me. All I could do was stand back and say WOW!!!, My harvest is so beautiful. On one hand I thought to myself, "Why didn't I do this 20 years ago? But on the other hand, I thought, "God did everything in His perfect time to be revealed for "Such a time as this." There it is. There's the Esther spirit. Esther was placed where she was for a reason bigger than she or anyone else could've ever imagined. She realized that she had a purpose. And when she was made aware of what she had to do, she made herself available. The assignment that Esther had was so dangerous that it could have gotten her killed. But she realized that her purpose was designed to do something that would make history. She said, "if I perish, I perish." She was willing to take risks and do whatever she had to do to fulfill her purpose. When I came to my crossroads, I knew that my purpose was bigger than me. I knew that what I had learned was for the masses. I knew that I needed to share this revelation that could transform lives. The W.O.W Effect needed to be administered to many who were plagued by the epidemic Toxic Word Syndrome. But there is a balm in Gilead. All I needed was the strength and the courage to make a stand for so many who didn't know that they had access to one of the most powerful tools ever. The nation of

Israel was redeemed from destruction because of Esther's courage. Just like Esther, God has a plan for my life and for your life too.

At this point I had to take inventory of my latest decade to put all the pieces together. There was a pattern of events that took place that I had never really acknowledged as significant until I arrived at this paradigm shift. There were seven deaths in this decade that were life altering for me. At the turn coming into my latest decade, 2008-2018, my brother Tim passed away. Three months later, one of my closest friends Lillie passed away. Four months after she died, my friend Ida passed away. And then five months after Ida, my father passed away. That was a lot in a brief period. I was turning the corner, pulling up weeds and tilling the soil, while dealing with loss at the same time. I knew more so than ever how short life was and that I needed to really start making the best of my time. You don't know where death is and every day that you live and breathe on this earth is precious. And I wanted to make sure that I fulfilled everything that there was for me to fulfill while I was still here. So, I went to work. I planted an awesome harvest of good seeds. I grew a sense of determination with a force to be reckoned with. But the most important thing that WOWed me was that I could finally do something I felt like I hadn't done in years. Breathe, sigh, and SMILE!!

This was an enjoyable time. I was free. I had ventured into a new business. I did a vision board for the first time ever. This was a part of my personal therapy. I began to sow words like Prosperity, Business Owner, Peace, Happiness, Love, Family, etc. So many areas of my life had been restored. Because in 2008 when I hit rock bottom, not only was I broken, but I was also broke, and homeless. This is something that even most of my family and closest friends didn't know – at least not until they pick up this book and read it from cover to cover. There was a season that I lived in my car and in a studio that I was working out of part time to save money for an apartment. I can't begin to tell you how many times Kyle called asking to come home, not knowing that there wasn't a home to come back to. I had to save every penny to move because I knew I had worn out my welcome at a friend's house. I did what I had to do. After getting into the house, the car I was driving was taken from me two months later. I was devastated, because I knew that I needed the car to get to my clients to make money. I told you my name, Anita, means God is gracious. Well God allowed me to find favor in my property owner and a friend who agreed to drive me around until I could get a car. He became my personal chauffeur. If it weren't for these two people, a lot of what I accomplished thereafter wouldn't have been possible. So, I am eternally grateful to Hiram and Leo. Even in that state, I was so happy to be free of the other issues, being driven around and being behind in my rent didn't bother me. They didn't bother me because I knew where I was headed. I knew that because of The W.O.W Effect, I would rise like a phoenix. I knew I was going to be more than fine.

Before long things had turned around so much, I started doing things that I had only dreamt of doing before. I took my sisters on their first cruise. This was the trip of a lifetime. Unbeknownst to them, I had upgraded our accommodations thanks to a promotion they were having. That allowed us to have the owner's suite. There were eight family members and two close friends on this trip. We had a blast. Suddenly I became compelled to do things out of the ordinary. I remodeled my mother's house. Her house had been the same since she built it in the early 1990s. It was such a joy to see the look on her face and the joy in her heart choosing paint colors and light fixtures. I celebrated her birthday in grand style every year with parties and family reunions and even trips. It made her so happy, and I enjoyed every minute of it. I enjoyed taking my sisters and nieces on shopping sprees. I enjoyed staying in a suite with my mother and sisters for her birthday weekend getaway. My mother had spent so much of her life taking care of everyone else, now it was her turn to be catered to. So, we did just that.

Five years into this journey, I got a call that my mother was not breathing and had no pulse and that my sister was administering CPR. My heart dropped to my stomach. I felt helpless. I lived four hours away. I was Miss Fix It. But I couldn't fix this. I was motionless when I got that call. I remember it like yesterday. I tried my best to stay calm. When I hung up the phone with my sister who was hysterical, I was preparing myself to hit the road. I said these words, "Lord please don't take her now, I'm not ready. She's healed. She will recover. She's not going to leave just yet. Ultimately, it's your will God." This was a powerful moment. The girl whose mouth had been so accustomed to spewing out the toxic words from her mind was now speaking words of hope and life. I made my request with also the acknowledgement that God's will be done. Wow! There's such a freedom in knowing that no matter what, you have the power to speak peace over any storm in your life just like Jesus did when He walked on water and said to the wind and the waves, "Peace! Be Still!'

For a whole week, my family and I were in limbo about my mother's frail condition. But after a week the ventilator was removed, and she was recovering. HALLELUJAH! What a miracle. Even her doctors were amazed. My sisters and I decided to relocate my mother. My sister Carrie, who had recently retired, my niece Alicia and I all decided to live together in a joint effort to manage her care. My sister Constance would make frequent trips to help and offer relief to us. It was a fun season, because we cared for mom and for the first time ever, she didn't call the shots. However, she lived like a queen. I will forever be grateful to God for allowing me to be able to take care of the woman who took care of so many. My mother was an extraordinarily strong woman with a huge heart. There wasn't a mouth she wouldn't feed. She took care of all her children and half of the kids in the neighborhood as well. When she saw a need, she just stepped in and took care of it. That was how people used to be. Neighbors helped each other and looked out for one another. We live in a different time now. All I wanted to do was to make sure she had the best care and that she could live in comfort and peace for the rest of her days. I had the most wonderful time living in peace and giving my mother the golden years that she deserved.

At the end of this decade, March to be exact, another close friend Allen died. This death devastated me. He was murdered. We felt robbed. Allen was a childhood friend. It's tough to lose someone you love so drastically. Me, Allen, and another friend who's like a sister, Melissa, were like The Three Musketeers. We were inseparable. Also, during this season, my mother's health was declining. Seven months later, my queen, the love of my life, my mother passed away. There are no words to describe the pain and void of losing a mother. I have good days and I have bad days. Even in my tears, I have coined a phrase spoken often by Bishop Victor T Curry, "We cry but we don't cry as though there is no hope." I know that I will always feel the effects of her loss, but one day it won't hurt as much. She lived a great life and in her last days, she didn't suffer. And the best part is that I know I will see her again. I know I did say seven deaths. Well, a month after my mother, I lost another close friend, Delfinia. At this time, I had no idea what the significance of these seven deaths were. But at the turn of 2018, it would start to become clear. Yes, there were seven deaths of people who held meaningful positions in my life. But the main thing is in the number. Seven is the number of completion. Now the most significant loss was my mother. Because this one left me feeling like I didn't know what to do or where to turn. I remember wondering, "What do I do now?" Then it hit me. It hit me ALL the way from 1968. Anita, you came into this world with a purpose so strong that toxic words tried to take you out. You have fought through so much adversity and you're still standing. You were broken and now you're whole. You were in turmoil now you have peace. You were broke now you're in business for yourself. All I could say was - W.O.W! Even in the loss of so many people that I loved; God brought about perfection. 7 - God's perfect number. At the turn of all this turbulence, was a new beginning; One with a new paradigm for a greater purpose than I had ever expected. Remember in 2008 I started producing devotionals and sending them out via email. I would always end with "Wow! Be Blessed and Be Free!" OMG this is what I'm supposed to do. I must share this. The words out of my own mouth have optimized my wholeness. I'm no longer this broken battered person. I'm whole now because of the power of positive words. This is what my whole life has meant. This is my purpose. This is what is on my new paradigm. God lined all of this up for such a time as this. W.O.W!

LIVING IN THE WOW

*T*HE WOW EFFECT HAS done its job. How does it feel to be free? Well, I can surely tell you that this freedom is rewarding. When in captivity, you eventually start to lose sight of life on the outside. I have watched many prison shows that helped me understand why there had to be a preparation season for them to adapt to a functional life in society. My life had gone through five decades of captivity. But once I was free, I would find myself tied up repeatedly, because I had not been rehabilitated. From a legal perspective I would have been labeled a "Habitual Criminal" not being able to function as a normal person in society without committing another crime.

This is so real to me. By the time I looked at myself, I mean really looked at myself; I didn't recognize me. I was lost beneath all the pain, and the battle wounds that had buried me in a shallow grave of 435pounds. Yes, I was 435 pounds when I woke up from this mental and emotional coma. Me! The one who was always very conscious of my physical well-being. I was that one who never ate junk food or partook of sugary drinks. I was the one who worked out every day without fail. To tell you the truth, I can't begin to tell you where that person went. I don't think I had even realized she was gone. Or I blocked out the fact that she'd ever existed. However, she was a mystery. She had become a figment of my imagination. Every decade that came with different situations, left behind a package that I now believe was designed by the enemy to set me up for an untimely demise.

I learned in my process of rehabilitation that when you optimize the words in your mind and change your thoughts, not only will you have a mindset transformation, but you will also transform physically. True transformation causes you to face ALL the ugly truths. How was it that I was able to ignore every warning sign from the threats of my obesity as if they weren't screaming," ANITA LOSE WEIGHT OR YOU WILL DIE!!!" I was experiencing inflammation and would quickly dismiss it by telling myself that I needed to put my feet up. Walking through an airport, I would get so winded that I would have to take pit stops and say that my backpack was too heavy. I won't dare start to talk about how many chairs and bed frames I'd broken over the years. I was even in denial about my high blood pressure and being pre diabetic. My life was a wreck. My credit score was super low. I could barely pay my bills. The stress level was through the roof. And it kept piling on and piling on. One of the things my mom said to me before she left this world was, "Don't stress yourself out and work yourself to death for nothing." I just brushed it off. I didn't want her to think I didn't have it under control. I was a hot mess. And then I woke up.

I didn't realize that the phrase WOW would enter my life again and have the impact it did. My own witty phrase is what saved my life. When I realized that only a mindset change and consistent work could solve all my issues, it became clear that God had provided me with the answer a decade sooner. I kept revisiting WOW over those ten years knowing that it was significant, but not understanding how to use it to change my situation. I was lying in my bed and rolled over on my phone and heard a lady sharing her story. That lady was Lisa Nichols of Motivating Masses. I had seen much of her work and had read a book by her years earlier. I saw her on the revolutionary mind transformation project, *The Secret*. I knew who she was, but there was something about her that day. I know now that it was a timely encounter that God had set up. As Lisa was talking, the tears were rolling down my face. I had recently gone through the death of my mother. I don't have any natural children, But I did raise my nephew Kyle as my own child. But still I had never felt so alone in the world at that time. I have a family, and I'm grateful. But there's something significant about having one or two people in the world that you know would go to the ends of the earth. I don't want my sisters Constance and Carrie to flip when they read this. I know you all are there for me always. But for those who have faced this moment in your life, you totally understand what I'm talking about. It's an eternal, life-altering event already; but when you are a single woman, you feel it differently.

While in my transformational phase, I sacrificed to go to Lisa Nichol's "Speak and Write to Make Millions" event in Orlando FL. It was the best three days I ever had. I had to pack my own food to eat in my room, but I did what was necessary for me to go. I heard what God was saying to me about this next phase in my life. I had to transform completely from the inside out. I left there so motivated to continue the things I had recently started. Everything I do transforms lives. As a vocal coach I'm helping people transform into the singers they desire to be. As a music industry consultant, I'm helping people transform into the music industry by helping them link to the right companies and individuals to fuel their agenda. As an author and public speaker, I'm able to help transform the lives of individuals speaking to get rid of their limiting beliefs and start living the best version of themselves. So, when Lisa posed the question to us, "What type of coach are you?" I knew beyond the shadow of a doubt that I was a transformational coach. Everything I do transforms lives. WOW!!! It's so good to find yourself underneath 435 pounds. Beneath the pounds, emerged a whole new person.

The 435-pound stronghold had my life, my purpose and my destiny locked up. I didn't realize it at the time, but in that state, I was not moving forward. I was going around in circles. The limiting beliefs that were brought on by TWS made me believe that I was born to be that way. Toxic words will cause you to self diagnose, because you're looking for the blame for why things are the way they are. Sadly, you don't want to accept the fact that the blame is looking back at you in the mirror. I can almost point to three 90-pound layers that I allowed myself to be buried under. My highest weight was 435 pounds. My ideal weight is between 145 and 150 pounds. That leaves roughly 270 pounds that I needed to lose. That's 90 times three! When I started to deal with my mindset as it related to my health,

I could easily point out three phases of my life that piled on those 270 pounds. My weight struggle didn't start until the third decade of my life. Each decade thereafter, I gained 90 lbs. This was the harshest reality I had to face. I had done this to myself. TWS was so bad that I allowed it to not only affect my mindset, but it had started to destroy me physically. When The W.O.W Effect started to work on my mindset, the scales fell off my eyes. I didn't recognize the 435-pound person staring back at me. I almost fell into depression. I had to shake myself and affirm myself out of the initial shock. I remember asking myself in the mirror, "Who are you? And what have you done with the real Anita?" I knew I had to deal with getting those layers off. I immediately started working on changing my mind about the myths and rhetoric of fad diets and conventional health care. A small group of friends, Brenda Jackson, Marilyn Magwood, and Angela Rowe and I started Eat Well Live Well Be Well LLC. (Thank you, ladies.) This saved my life. Not only am I able to help myself transform and take my life back but I am able to help others do the same. I remember how liberated I felt when I got the first layer of 90 pounds off. I could get a glimpse of the person I was before the layers of pain, depression, fatigue, and doubt had wrapped around me. I was finally on my way to truly living life in the W.O.W!

My transformation started to bring about such a meaningful change in how I lived, interacted, and functioned. Not only am I feeling great mentally, but I started shedding the extra baggage. Who knew it would feel this good to lose weight? All of this is a result of this wonderful anecdote that I pray you will allow yourself to apply to your life. I am living in the W.O.W! For so long, I was living a fraction of myself, as most of us do. I wish it hadn't taken me so long to figure it all out. But the one thing I'm certainly glad about is that I was able to come out of that shallow grave and live again. Words really do optimize wholeness. You can reinvent your life by changing the way you think. As I say so often, when we think better, we speak better and when we speak better, we live better. The right words coming out of your mouth can move mountains. I talked about it and sang about it for so long, but I really didn't believe it or live it. But it's a new day. I want that for every single person whose eyes will park on these pages. There's no way I could keep this to myself. I had to share it with the world because I know that there are so many people experiencing what I experienced.

I'm now in a much better place. No, I'm not perfect and life does have its challenges; but I have a new way of sorting out my thoughts and being slow to speak. I take some time and meditate. I repeat my mantra "I will boldly and freely live my truth!" There's healing and deliverance in my stories. There's no way I could put all my life and the lessons I learned into one book; but sharing the W.O.W Effect with you is a pleasure for me. I know it works and many others have shared their testimonies. I'm determined to have the rest of my years be so much better than the former. So, I boldly declare to live the best version of Anita without fail. Now you go and do the same. WOW! Be Blessed and Be Free!